CONTENTS

Royal Navy Yearbook

Subs – Carriers – Frigates – Marines – Fly Navy

Royal Navy in 2024
- 4 Welcome
- 6 First Sea Lord Sets Course: The Royal Navy's leader talks tough
- 10 Sailors, Ships and Kit: In the news

On Operations
- 16 Red Sea Battles: HMS *Diamond* and HMS *Richmond* in action
- 22 Lebanon and Gaza: On station in the eastern Med
- 24 On NATO Duty: Operation Steadfast Defender off Norway
- 26 Royal Marines Down Under: Commandos exercise in the outback
- 28 Around the World Tour: Patrol vessels in the Pacific
- 29 Watching The Gulf: HMS *Lancaster* on duty
- 30 HMS *Prince of Wales* enters the drone era: Aviation trials on our newest carrier
- 34 Propeller Trouble: What is wrong with our carriers?

On This Day
- 40 Battle of the River Plate: The first naval action of World War Two
- 42 The Longest Day: The Royal Navy and D-Day
- 44 Allied Naval Power: 75 years of the Royal Navy and NATO

Submarine Service
- 46 The Silent Service: The Royal Navy's underwater battle force
- 48 New Dreadnought: Britain's first nuclear-powered submarine
- 50 Barrow-in-Furness: Home of Britain's nuclear submarines
- 54 Tomahawk Shooters: Royal Navy sub operations 1990 to 2024
- 58 New Nuclear Deterrent: The new HMS *Dreadnought*

The Fleet Today
- 62 Britain's Naval Power: The Royal Navy fleet in 2024
- 64 Submarine Force: Bombers and attack boats
- 68 The Carriers: HMS *Queen Elizabeth* and HMS *Prince of Wales*
- 70 Defending the Fleet: Type 45 Destroyers
- 72 Workhorses of the Fleet: Type 23 Frigates
- 75 Specialist Ships: Assault ships, mine countermeasures, and patrol vessels
- 81 Supporting the Fleet: Tankers, landing ships and underwater operations
- 86 Fly Navy: Jets, sub hunters, Junglies, and drones
- 94 Commando Force: Amphibious warriors and more

Royal Navy Future
- 102 Showing the Flag: The Royal Navy heads to the Pacific
- 106 Future Fleet: New warships and subs
- 110 Stormy Seas Ahead: Royal Navy faces new challenges

TOP: Britain's two Queen Elizabeth-class aircraft carriers are now dominating Royal Navy operations. (MOD CROWN COPYRIGHT)

ABOVE: River-class offshore patrol boats are now on duty in the Pacific, South Atlantic and Caribbean. (MOD CROWN COPYRIGHT)

LEFT: Each winter Royal Marines train above the Arctic Circle in northern Norway. (MOD CROWN COPYRIGHT)

FAR LEFT: The Royal Navy is soon to receive the final two of its seven Astute-class nuclear powered attack submarines. (MOD CROWN COPYRIGHT)

ISBN: 978 1 83632 015 9
Editor: Tim Ripley
Data and photo research: Fergus Ripley
Senior editor, specials: Roger Mortimer
Email: roger.mortimer@keypublishing.com
Cover Design: Steve Donovan
Design: SJmagic DESIGN SERVICES, India
Advertising Sales Manager: Sam Clark
Email: sam.clark@keypublishing.com
Tel: 01780 755131

Advertising Production: Becky Antoniades
Email: Rebecca.antoniades@keypublishing.com

SUBSCRIPTIONS/MAIL ORDER
Key Publishing Ltd, PO Box 300, Stamford, Lincs, PE9 1NA
Tel: 01780 480404
Subscriptions email: subs@keypublishing.com
Mail Order email: orders@keypublishing.com

Website: www.keypublishing.com/shop

PUBLISHING
Group CEO and Publisher: Adrian Cox

Published by
Key Publishing Ltd, PO Box 100, Stamford, Lincs, PE9 1XQ
Tel: 01780 755131
Website: www.keypublishing.com

PRINTING
Precision Colour Printing Ltd, Haldane, Halesfield 1, Telford, Shropshire. TF7 4QQ

DISTRIBUTION
Seymour Distribution Ltd, 2 Poultry Avenue, London, EC1A 9PU
Enquiries Line: 02074 294000.

We are unable to guarantee the bona fides of any of our advertisers. Readers are strongly recommended to take their own precautions before parting with any information or item of value, including, but not limited to money, manuscripts, photographs, or personal information in response to any advertisements within this publication. © Key Publishing Ltd 2024 All rights reserved. No part of this magazine may be reproduced or transmitted in any form by any means, electronic or mechanical, including photocopying, recording or by any information storage and retrieval system, without prior permission in writing from the copyright owner. Multiple copying of the contents of the magazine without prior written approval is not permitted.

INTRODUCTION

Welcome

The Royal Navy in 2024

RIGHT: The Royal Navy's last remaining Trafalgar-class submarine, HMS Triumph, will have to remain in service until the last two Astute-class boats are completed which is expected by 2026. (MOD CROWN COPYRIGHT)

Welcome to the latest edition of Key Publishing's *Royal Navy Yearbook*, which aims to profile the current state of Britain's naval service, review its activities over the past year and look forward to future challenges.

The Royal Navy traces its history back to the days of King Henry VIII, when the famous Tudor monarch founded Britain's first standing navy in 1545. It was initially known as the 'Navy Royal' but soon the term 'Royal Navy' came into common use.

After Sir Francis Drake defeated the Spanish Amanda in 1588, an unprecedented era of English and then British naval expansion took place. Admiral Horatio Nelson's victory at Trafalgar in 1805 set the stage for more than a century of naval supremacy that coincided with the global expansion of the British Empire.

Today the Royal Navy operates in a completely different geo-political and military environment. Britain is part of the NATO alliance and is pledged to defend its 31 allies around Europe and in North America. Britain retains responsibilities to defend and secure overseas territories in the Caribbean, South Atlantic, Mediterranean, and Indian Ocean. As a permanent member of the United Nations Security Council, Britain is often called upon to support peacekeeping and other international missions to sustain peace and security around the world.

All these missions require strong armed forces, often involving naval assets, to deter aggression and respond to outbreaks of armed conflict, as well as supporting peacekeeping and humanitarian missions.

At the same time, the Royal Navy is responsible for providing Britain's independent nuclear deterrent, keeping a Trident missile armed Vanguard-class nuclear submarine at sea, 24/7/365. Continuous at sea deterrent patrols have been undertaken since 1968, as Britain's ultimate guarantee of national survival.

In this edition of the *Royal Navy Yearbook,* we look back at the important contribution the Senior Service has made to keeping international sea lanes open in the Red Sea in the face of missile and drone attacks by Houthi rebels based in Yemen.

We also take a special look at the role of the Royal Navy's submarine

BELOW: Wings of the sea. A Merlin helicopter of the Fleet Air Arm pops flares during NATO's Exercise Steadfast Defender. (MOD CROWN COPYRIGHT)

INTRODUCTION

LEFT: The new HMS *Cardiff* is soon to be put into the water at BAE Systems' shipyard on the Clyde. (BAE SYSTEMS)

service, including profiling the nation's first nuclear powered submarine, HMS *Dreadnought* which was decommissioned in 1980 and the shipyard at Barrow-in-Furness where Britain's nuclear submarines are built. We also profile the new HMS *Dreadnought*. Currently under construction, it will be the first of the Royal Navy's new class of nuclear deterrent submarines.

The status of the Royal Navy's current fleet of warships and Royal Fleet Auxiliary support ships is profiled, and we highlight the Fleet Air Arms' squadrons and commando units of the Royal Marines. In conclusion, we look forward to the Royal Navy's major deployment to the Far East next year, look at the progress of efforts to bring new warships into service and examine the challenges facing British naval power.

We hope you find the *Royal Navy Yearbook* informative and that it helps increase knowledge and understanding of Britain's naval service in the 21st century.

Tim Ripley
Editor
Royal Navy Yearbook

LEFT: Naval top brass. The Royal Navy's senior leadership faces tough challenges in coming years. (TIM RIPLEY)

BELOW: Tim Ripley on the ski jump of HMS *Prince of Wales*. (TIM RIPLEY)

 **DON'T MISS OUT ON OTHER KEY MILITARY MAGAZINE SPECIALS**
If you'd like information about Key Publishing's military books, magazine specials, subscription offers and the latest product releases sent directly to your inbox. **Scan here »**

NAVY AT WORK

First Sea Lord Sets Course

The Royal Navy's leader talks tough

ABOVE: The Royal Navy's fleet is showing signs of its age and keeping his warships in action is a priority for Admiral Sir Ben Key. (MOD CROWN COPYRIGHT)

Britain's naval leadership was on the road earlier this year spreading the word about the importance of naval power to the country and pushing for the Royal Navy to change to meet new challenges. Speaking in May at the First Sea Lord's Sea Power Conference 2024, in London, Admiral Sir Ben Key made the case for the Royal Navy to up its game to counter new and evolving threats, often close to home.

The head of the Royal Navy told the conference, "No doubt speakers will allude to [the fact that we live in challenging times] throughout the rest of the day and tomorrow. That is not a surprise. Global instability is on the rise, the world is changing faster, all of these are well established truths."

RIGHT: Admiral Sir Ben Key travelled to Australia in July 2024 to meet his Australian and US counterparts to monitor progress on the AUKUS submarine programme. (MOD CROWN COPYRIGHT)

6 ROYAL NAVY YEARBOOK 2024–25

He was speaking just after former Prime Minister Rishi Sunak had committed to raising defence spending to 2.5% of GDP by the end of the decade, with Sir Ben saying: "it is very welcome, it is very timely, and I believe it is going to be a genuinely catalytic moment. Because it allows us, both with defence, but also our defence industry partners and more broadly to set plans and programmes going ahead...with a confidence of financial commitment that allows us to make the long-term changes that we really need to make."

"As many of us have discussed over recent years, when you're operating in a time of feast and famine those long-term plans can be very difficult to generate with confidence, and the risk picture shifts to one of caution," he said. "With the world we're in at the moment we cannot afford that cautious approach, we cannot afford that short term thinking. What it actually demands from us is something that accelerates the speed in which we do things."

LEFT: Admiral Sir Ben Key has been First Sea Lord since November 2021. (MOD CROWN COPYRIGHT)

"And in going faster, inevitably, we have to be more comfortable with our concepts of risk," said Sir Ben. "In order to be comfortable with risk and investment opportunities we therefore need a security of funding going ahead. So, I genuinely mean it when I say as head of the Royal Navy alongside my fellow service chiefs. This is a very welcome announcement."

"But the solution space as no doubt we'll discuss over the next few days isn't one that just sits within defence and as I mentioned very briefly earlier, it is something that we need to establish across the nation," he said. "When Prime Minister

BELOW: The Royal Navy's two Queen Elizabeth-class aircraft carriers are the centre of its surface operations in support of NATO and further afield. (MOD CROWN COPYRIGHT)

NAVY AT WORK

ABOVE: Building the Royal Navy's next generation of nuclear submarines is proving to be an engineering, project management and financial challenge.
(BAE SYSTEMS)

[Sunak] launched the recent demand paper talking about the nuclear deterrent as a national endeavour, this was something really unusual in recent times. Because it was an overt commitment or conversation about what it means to be a nuclear weapon owning nation and there are few of us in the world and only three in NATO...that it also got out into the open what it means to invest properly as a national endeavour into delivering our security."

"I pay tribute to my colleague, Maddy McTernan, Chief of Defence Nuclear, who has done so much with her cross-government connectivity to drive this forward. But actually, it's a maritime conversation. It's not just a nuclear conversation. It's one that talks about how the fabric of this great nation will pull together all of its strengths, all of its talents...to ensure that everything that extends from our coastline and going ahead, is secure, is resilient and are designed around our economic prosperity. And so, we are working as a navy and defence across business industry, charities, the Royal National Lifeboat Institute, to maximise our ability to monitor and defend our interests at sea. Those interests always used to be thought of as being abroad and afar."

"People say we never see the Royal Navy. Well, that's because we're over the horizon. We were permanently playing an away game. We're gone, we're deployed too far off seas."

"But actually, that threat is moving ever present and ever closer and as we've seen from the Nord Stream

NAVY AT WORK

Two gas [pipeline] attacks [in the Baltic Sea] that occurred a few years ago, actually we can be challenged almost in our back waters as Norway found," he said.

"And the Norwegian response was really instructive. Because what they did was pull together commerce, government, defence, to construct a coordinated and coherent response to this play. Recognising that no one part of the Norwegian ecosystem could deliver that answer but working together they could produce something so much more resilient."

"I believe that is the sort of a model that we could take so much from and take forward," he said. "We have a part to play in that and the [underwater surveillance ship] RFA *Proteus* is just one example of how we are trying to break some of the old paradigms and set up some new ones. The ship was bought within year of the idea being generated. We didn't design it from scratch. We saw what was available on the market. ... Agile, adaptable fail fast, learn more, move on. And this is part of the broader response."

"None of our response can be delivered without the extraordinary efforts of the sailors and marines that I am privileged to lead across the Naval Service," he said. "Regulars, reservists and our wonderful civil service and industrial partners. And also, the families who support them. There are some who are putting up with quite extraordinary sacrifice at the moment and I pay tribute to them. And what we have to do is to forge ahead and to demonstrate that actually we are building a new and better Royal Navy."

"It needs to be better because the challenges are going to be more considerable," said Sir Ben. "It's going to be new because many of our ships and platforms are getting older. That's a truth. No doubt you can challenge it, but it is what it is. And we need to be able to demonstrate that we are responding and making the step change into the future that the nation would expect, and that the government has charged me and my colleagues on the Navy Board to lead."

FIRST SEA LORD – ADMIRAL SIR BEN KEY

Sir Ben was educated at Bromsgrove School and joined the Royal Navy in 1984 as a University Cadet, subsequently graduating in Physics from Royal Holloway, University of London. He qualified as both helicopter aircrew and as a principal warfare officer and as a junior officer saw service around the world in a variety of frigates and destroyers. He commanded the aircraft carrier HMS *Illustrious* from 2009 to 2010. Promoted to Vice Admiral in February 2016, he was the Royal Navy's fleet commander from then until March 2019. He then served as the chief of joint operations, prior to his appointment as First Sea Lord in November 2021. Ben and his wife Elly have three children and make their home in Dorset.

The First Sea Lord is the professional head of the Royal Navy and a member of the Defence Council. He is responsible to the secretary of state for the fighting effectiveness, efficiency, and morale of His Majesty's Naval Service. As a member of the Chiefs of Staff Committee, he advises the chief of defence staff on maritime strategy and policy.

Admiral Sir Ben Key is the British government's senior naval advisor and a strong advocate of sea power.
(MOD CROWN COPYRIGHT)

LEFT: The Royal Navy is progressively modernising its fleet of warships, submarines, and support vessels, as well as its aircraft and helicopters.
(MOD CROWN COPYRIGHT)

IN THE NEWS

Sailors, Ships and Kit

In the News

New Addition to the Fleet

ABOVE: The Duke of Edinburgh led the dedication of RFA *Stirling Castle* in the Royal Fleet Auxiliary in May 2024.
(MOD CROWN COPYRIGHT)

IN MAY 2024, the Duke of Edinburgh led the dedication service of a new Royal Fleet Auxiliary ship which will help safeguard British waters from underwater threats.

Resplendent in her unique blue and white livery, the RFA *Stirling Castle* was formally dedicated during the high-profile ceremony at HM Naval Base Clyde at Faslane.

The entry of the ship into service marks a move away from traditional mine hunting, embracing cutting-edge technology as she acts as a 'mother ship' for an array of remotely operated and autonomous systems which will scour home waters looking for mines.

RFA *Stirling Castle* is now working with experts from the Royal Navy's Mine Threat Exploitation Group (MTXG) at Faslane. Its Zulu Squadron is at the forefront of advancing new mine hunting technologies, helping the Royal Navy to keep pace with the evolving threat from underwater naval mines. Some of the new, high-tech equipment includes autonomous surface vessels and uncrewed underwater vehicles (UUVs) capable of being operated remotely using a portable command centre.

Her commanding officer, Captain Duncan Vernoum RFA, hailed his ship as "a highly capable vessel with a highly trained and motivated ship's company. In concert with embarked Royal Navy mission teams and specialist personnel, the ship is at the forefront of the Royal Navy's future mine hunting capability. There is more work to be done to achieve full operational capability and this will take place in the next few months."

His ship began life as oil rig support vessel MV *Island Crown* but was snapped up by the Royal Navy in 2023 and underwent extensive conversion at Devonport naval base to transform her into the first RFA vessel dedicated to supporting mine hunting.

RIGHT: RFA *Stirling Castle* will help the Royal Navy transition into a fully autonomous mine counter-measures force.
(MOD CROWN COPYRIGHT)

IN THE NEWS

Royal Seal of Approval

HMS *VENTURER*, the Royal Navy's newest frigate, was visited in Rosyth dockyard by her new royal sponsor, The Princess Royal.

Princess Anne met those responsible for constructing the UK's first Type 31 frigate, as well as the sailors charged with breathing life into the 455-foot-long vessel and turning her into a working warship ready to serve around the globe.

Venturer is the latest Royal Navy warship to be sponsored by The Princess Royal – who is also royal sponsor of Devonport-based assault ship HMS *Albion*. The Princess Royal is also commodore-in-chief of Portsmouth Naval Base and chief commandant of women in the Royal Navy among numerous long-standing associations with the Senior Service.

LEFT: Members of the Royal Family take a close interest in the wellbeing of the ships of the Royal Navy and their crews. As ship's sponsor, The Princess Royal looks after the interests of HMS *Venturer*.
(MOD CROWN COPYRIGHT)

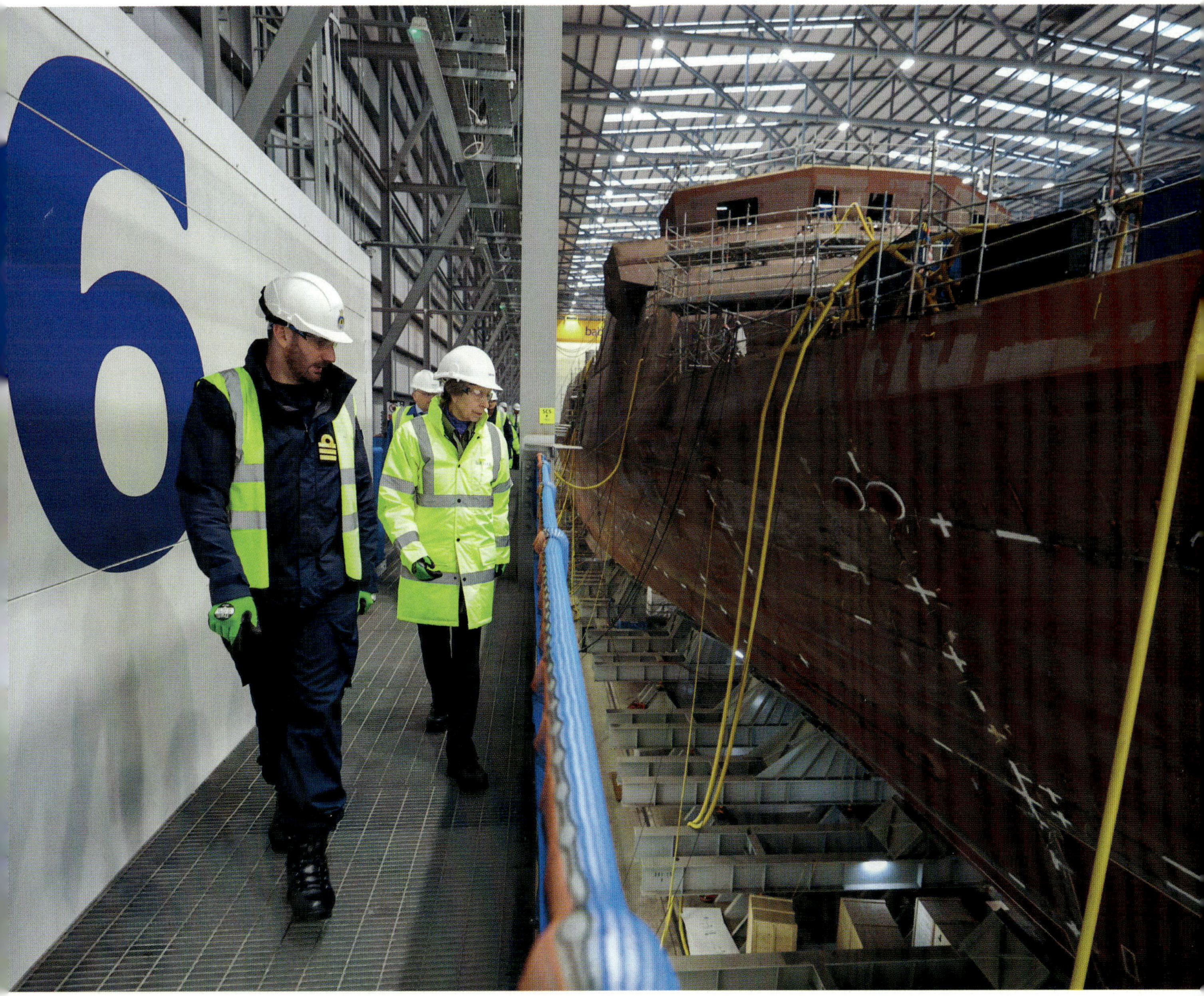

BELOW: The Prince Royal visited HMS *Venturer* in April 2024 to inspect progress on the construction.
(MOD CROWN COPYRIGHT)

www.keymilitary.com II

IN THE NEWS

Aussie Nuclear Officers

ABOVE: Three Royal Australian Navy officers have graduated from the Royal Navy's nuclear engineering school at HMS *Sultan* in Gosport.
(MOD CROWN COPYRIGHT)

THREE ROYAL Australian Navy officers are among the first in their service's history to qualify as nuclear engineers.

After nine months of intensive training at HMS *Sultan* in Gosport they will now serve alongside their Royal Navy counterparts in British submarines.

They will then go on to help develop Australia's nuclear submarine capability as part of the AUKUS agreement between the UK, USA, and Australia.

Named only as Lieutenant Commander James, Lieutenant Isabella, and Lieutenant Steve, the trio will now go on to serve in Astute-class submarines alongside Royal Navy crews, adding practical experience to all they have learned on the Nuclear Operator Course.

Their success marks a significant milestone in developing the skilled workforce to operate Australia's future nuclear powered submarine capability.

On the Bridge

NEW VIRTUAL reality simulators have been installed by the Royal Navy at bases in England and Scotland.

The nine hi-tech bridge simulators – which accurately recreate both the bridge of present-day warships, but also the key waters and harbours they operate in – have been installed at sites in England and Scotland, with the Royal Navy's warfare school at HMS *Collingwood* in Fareham being the first to benefit.

The £27 million investment, delivered by a consortium led by Capita, in partnership with Metaverse VR and serving Royal Navy personnel, is intended to make learning navigation and running a bridge more realistic, more comprehensive, and potentially faster.

Five simulator suites have been installed at HMS *Collingwood*: two large 'full mission' simulators with wrap-around digital display screens and virtual reality headsets, a smaller version with an LCD display and finally two small trainers – more akin to a video gaming set-up, but with the same features and accuracy as their full-size counterparts. Sailors put on headsets on the mock-up bridge wing – and suddenly they are immersed in a 3D world.

Trainee warfare officer Sub Lieutenant Stephen Smallman said: "The old simulator was good, but you knew you were in a room with some screens. Here, you feel like you are stepping onto the bridge of a warship. It is very easy to become immersed in the situation – it makes everything feel much more real."

RIGHT: Trainee Royal Navy bridge crews are now using virtual reality technology to learn their essential skills.
(MOD CROWN COPYRIGHT)

IN THE NEWS

New Order For Missiles

AN ORDER for an unidentified number of Lightweight Multirole Missiles (LMM) has been placed with Thales UK in Belfast for the supply of the versatile, precision weapon to the Royal Navy and British Army. The order, worth £176m will equip current and future short-range air defence capabilities for the British Army, such as Stormer combat vehicles, and be fired by the Royal Navy's Martlet maritime anti-surface missile system on Wildcat helicopters.

The Royal Navy uses the LMM to provide a precision solution against threats such as drones, helicopters, other aircraft, and small, fast maritime targets. LMM were first fired from a Wildcat in the Bay of Bengal during the Royal Navy's Carrier Strike Group deployment of 2021, marking initial operating capability for the Martlet system. Martlet has since supported operations including Operation Prosperity Guardian, helping to protect commercial ships from attacks by Houthi rebels in the Red Sea.

BELOW: The Thales Martlet missile equips Royal Navy Wildcat HMA2 maritime helicopters. (MOD CROWN COPYRIGHT)

New Raiders

A REVAMPED raiding boat, the Commando Raiding Craft (CRC), has entered service with the Royal Marines.

The CRC is a redesigned version of the tried-and-tested Offshore Raiding Craft – commonly known as the ORC.

After two decades' service with the Royal Marines around the globe, it's been given an overhaul to meet the demands of the commandos in the mid-21st century as they return to their World War Two raiding roots: coastal landings behind enemy lines with small teams wreaking havoc on enemy infrastructure and systems.

Repainted in grey to help concealment, the CRC also has new engines providing increased range – more than 200 nautical miles – and increased speed – up to 40kts – and a new configuration with driving position moved forwards from the stern for better manoeuvrability.

The commanding officer of the Plymouth-based 47 Commando, Colonel William Norcott, said: "The CRC is multi-purpose and more supportive of the Commando Force model, working in small, disaggregated teams that are structured to deliver a lethal punch. We are really excited to have something that does what it says on the tin."

BELOW: The Commando Force is now operating the Commando Raiding Craft for amphibious raiding behind enemy lines. (MOD CROWN COPYRIGHT)

IN THE NEWS

Caribbean Drugs Busts

ROYAL NAVY warship, HMS *Trent* seized more than £40m-worth of cocaine in the Caribbean Sea during a drugs bust in August.

The River-class off-shore patrol vessel has successfully completed six drugs busts in 2024, taking close to seven tons of drugs worth £551.5m from drug traffickers. In this operation on August 8, 2024 – her first since April, HMS *Trent* was alerted to a speed boat that was suspected to be smuggling cocaine around 120nm south of the Dominican Republic.

With a US Navy maritime patrol aircraft flying overhead, the Portsmouth-based warship closed in and dispatched the Royal Marines and US Coast Guard on board to intercept the vessel. The smugglers threw their cargo overboard during the operation, but thanks to HMS *Trent*'s swift response all contraband was seized. The 506kg of Class A narcotics were seized, and three smugglers were handed over to the United States authorities for prosecution.

HMS *Trent*'s commanding officer, Commander Tim Langford, said: "This successful operation with our American partners demonstrates HMS *Trent*'s ability to support anti-trafficking operations in the Caribbean Sea. Every member of my team can be proud of another significant haul – the sixth this year.

"These successful interceptions disrupt Transnational Criminal Organisations (TCO) and underscore the Royal Navy's vital role in maintaining maritime security and upholding international law both at home and abroad."

LEFT: Three drug smugglers were arrested during the August 2024 bust and handed over to the US Coast Guard.
(MOD CROWN COPYRIGHT)

BELOW: Boarding parties from HMS *Trent* seized $40m worth of cocaine from a small craft in the Caribbean in August, 2024.
(MOD CROWN COPYRIGHT)

Watching the Dragon

THE ROYAL Navy warship HMS *Richmond* kept a close watch on a Chinese Navy task group as it passed the UK twice in three weeks.

The Plymouth-based Type 23 frigate monitored the People's Liberation Army Navy ships first as they headed to St Petersburg in Russia to participate in that country's Navy Days events in July 2024.

Working alongside NATO allies, the British warship was on hand to keep the two Chinese vessels – the PLANS *Jiaozuo*, a 7500-tonne destroyer, and PLANS *Honghu*, a 23,400-tonne supply ship – under surveillance as they made their return journey through the North Sea and into the Channel, travelling through UK waters under a routine rite of passage.

Although the presence of Chinese Navy ships in the English Channel is not common, it's not the first time the Royal Navy has maintained watch on Chinese ships heading to or from the Russian city for its annual naval gathering. HMS *St Albans* and HMS *Westminster* were called on to monitor the Chinese destroyer PLANS *Xian* as it sailed to and from the same event in 2019.

HMS *Richmond* took over from the French ship FS *Commandant Blaison* which maintained contact with the Chinese duo past its country's coastline.

The British warship maintained contact from there until reaching the North Sea, where Belgian Navy patrol ship BNS *Pollux* continued to follow PLANS *Jiaozuo* and PLANS *Honghu*.

HMS *Richmond's* commanding officer, Commander Richard Kemp, said:

"Close monitoring of foreign vessels in UK waters is routine business for the Royal Navy and ensures their compliance with maritime law and respect for UK sovereignty.

By maintaining a visible and persistent presence, the Royal Navy demonstrates our commitment to the NATO alliance and in maintaining maritime security which is crucial to our national interests."

A fortnight later, HMS *Richmond* assumed monitoring duties again, taking over from the Belgians once more, this time patrol ship BNS *Castor* as the Chinese vessels made a beeline for the Dover Strait on their return journey from the Baltic Sea.

ABOVE: HMS *Richmond* was twice scrambled in July to escort Chinese warships transiting the English Channel. (MOD CROWN COPYRIGHT)

BELOW: The Chinese destroyer PLANS *Jiaozuo* (top) and support vessel PLANS *Honghu* (centre) move through the English Channel, monitored by HMS *Richmond's* Merlin HM2 helicopter. (MOD CROWN COPYRIGHT)

ON OPERATIONS

Red Sea Battles

HMS *Diamond* and HMS *Richmond* in Action

ABOVE: HMS *Diamond* returned to Portsmouth sporting 10 kill markings representing the missiles and drones she shot down over the Red Sea.
(MOD CROWN COPYRIGHT)

When Hamas fighters breached Israel's border wall around the Gaza Strip on October 7, 2023, it set off a chain of events that rapidly escalated into a conflict across the Middle East. The following day, US President Joe Biden ordered two US Navy carrier battlegroups to gather in the Middle East in a show of force to deter other regional powers getting involved in the Gaza war.

Houthi rebels in Yemen quickly declared their support for the Palestinians in Gaza and said they would attack any Israeli ships in the Red Sea. On October 19, 2023, USS *Carney,* on patrol off Yemen, shot down four cruise missiles and 15 drones over a period of nine hours. Within weeks, attacks on merchant shipping in the Red Sea were happening on a daily basis.

In London, the British government soon decided to join the US operation to ensure the freedom of navigation for merchant ships in the Red Sea. The Royal Navy prepared one of its Type 45 destroyers, HMS *Diamond*, to sail to join Operation Prosperity Guard, as the Americans were now calling the Red Sea mission.

On November 19, 2023, the Japanese owned car transporter, the MV *Galaxy Leader* was boarded by a team of Houthi commandos, who landed on her by helicopter off the coast of Yemen. The crisis was now escalating dramatically. Three days later HMS *Diamond* sailed from Portsmouth en route to the Red Sea, under her

RIGHT: View from the bridge. A Sea Viper missile is launched from HMS *Diamond* **on January 9, 2024. This is the iconic image of the destroyer's Red Sea deployment.**
(MOD CROWN COPYRIGHT)

ON OPERATIONS

ABOVE: On April 24, HMS *Diamond* successful shot down a Houthi ballistic missile in the first ever engagement of its type by the British armed forces. (MOD CROWN COPYRIGHT)

commanding officer, Commander Pete Evans. The ship would be away from her home port for eight months and during that time would see the most intense period of combat for any Royal Navy warship since the 1991 Gulf War. That was the last time a British warship successfully engaged enemy missiles, when the Type 42 destroyer HMS *Gloucester* shot down an Iraqi Silkworm anti-ship missile heading towards the USS *Missouri*. HMS *Diamond*'s period of combat in the Red Sea would match the intensity last seen in the 1982 Falklands conflict.

After logistic and training stops at the British naval base on Gibraltar and the US Navy base at Souda Bay on Crete, HMS *Diamond* headed through the Suez Canal on December 14 and entered the Prosperity Guardian operational area.

It was not long before HMS *Diamond* was in action and on December 15, she used her Sea Viper missile system to shoot down a Houthi drone heading towards a merchant ship. It was the first time the weapon system had been used in action and from all accounts it worked perfectly. The crew were at action stations in the white anti-flash uniforms during the engagement and officers on the destroyer had only a few seconds to decide to fire at targets. Code names were soon assigned for the different threats, with drones being called 'cyclops', ballistic missiles called 'fireballs' and conventional missiles known as 'Zippos'.

The allied naval command did not use warships, such as HMS *Diamond* to escort convoys of merchant ships through the Red Sea but positioned their assets to defend 'patrol boxes', which the warships were expected to keep safe from attack. HMS *Diamond* also took turns to be the Sector Air Defence Commander (SADC) for the Red Sea region, co-ordinating communications and allocating other allied warships to engage targets as threats emerged. This set the scene for future engagements in the Red Sea.

Over Christmas and New Year, HMS *Diamond* remained on station as Houthi attacks with aerial drones, ballistic missiles, anti-ship missiles and robot boats escalated. HMS *Diamond* was caught up in these engagements on January 9, 2024, when she shot down seven Houthi drones in one day. This was the largest number of airborne targets shot down by a British warship since World War Two. The British destroyer was operating in concert with US warships that came under attack by 21 Houthi cruise and ballistic missiles. One of the drones was »

LEFT: Houthi attacks with missiles, drones, and robot boats have played havoc with merchant shipping in the Red Sea and prompted shipping lines to re-route their vessels around the Cape of Good Hope to avoid the war zone. (US CENTCOM)

ON OPERATIONS

ABOVE: HMS *Diamond* took on fuel and supplies from US Navy replenishment ships during her operations in the Red Sea. (MOD CROWN COPYRIGHT)

BELOW: The USS *Dwight D Eisenhower* provided air cover for HMS *Diamond* and HMS *Richmond* during their patrols in the Red Sea. (US NAVY)

shot down by the destroyer's 30mm Automated Small Calibre Gun in the first confirmed gun kill against an aerial target since the Korean war in the 1950s.

The engagement was caught on camera by Royal Navy photographers who released dramatic images of the Sea Viper missiles being launched at night from the destroyers forward vertical launch cells. The crew of HMS *Diamond* spent days at a time, at defence watches, in flash gear and manning every weapon system. When missiles or drones were detected heading towards the Red Sea, the ships command staff would issue the warning 'brace, brace, brace' over the public address system.

The attacks were growing in terms of weapons and their regularity, so the British and US governments decided to up the ante. Two days later the Royal Air Force joined with the US Navy to launch a wave of air strikes against Houthi missile and drone launch sites. Engagements were coming thick and fast now, as HMS *Diamond* took turns with US warships to patrol dedicated areas in the Red Sea to allow them to protect merchant ships. Later in January a further two Houthi drones were shot down by the destroyer.

HMS *Diamond* had now used up so many of her Sea Viper air defence missiles that she had to be withdrawn from the combat zone to re-arm. The vertical launch cells on Type 45s can only be re-loaded while the ship is stationary in a port using specialist cranes. So, *Diamond* had to return to Gibraltar to take on a full combat load of new missiles. Essential maintenance was also scheduled to keep the ship in fighting condition. When the ship arrived in Gibraltar, she sported nine kill markings painted on the side of her bridge to record her battle successes.

In the first week of February, the Type 23 frigate HMS *Richmond* arrived in the Red Sea to temporarily relieve

ON OPERATIONS

ABOVE: US Navy F/A-18E/F Super Hornet jets led a series of strikes against Houthi positions in Yemen from January 2024. (US NAVY)

HMS *Diamond*, while she headed to Gibraltar. It was not long before she got a taste of action when the Houthi fired a mass barrage of 57 missiles and drones at the allied naval force off the coast of Yemen. This was the largest swarm attack of the conflict to date.

HMS *Richmond* used its Sea Ceptor missiles to shoot down two attack drones during this engagement, in the first operational use of the weapon. She remained on station for another week before heading for home after a successful period in the Red Sea that included moving to provide assistance to a merchant ship hit by a Houthi missile and deploying boarding parties to search seven vessels for arms being smuggled into Yemen.

On March 2, HMS *Diamond* had completed her re-arming and headed back to the Red Sea to return to the action. The Houthis were still firing missiles and drones at merchant ships and allied warships, despite repeated allied air and missile strikes on their launch positions.

In another first for the destroyer, it shot down a Houthi anti-ship ballistic missile on April 24 in the first ever engagement of a ballistic missile by the British armed forces. This would be the last kill claimed by the destroyer during its mission.

The destroyer remained on station in the Red Sea during May and into June, protecting merchant ships and also conducting boarding operations against small craft suspected of smuggling arms to the Houthis.

HMS *Diamond* also became embroiled in the propaganda war between the allies and the Houthis, as well as their Iranian allies. Twice the Houthis claimed to have sunk the destroyer, and the Iranian government imposed unspecified 'sanctions' against her captain, as well as the commanding officer of HMS *Richmond*.

»

BELOW: RAF Typhoon jets based on Cyprus joined the US Navy air strikes on Yemen in January 2024. (MOD CROWN COPYRIGHT)

www.keymilitary.com 19

ON OPERATIONS

By mid-June, HMS *Diamond*'s tour of duty was over, and she headed for home, arriving back in the UK on July 6 after sailing 44,000 miles during her deployment. At the end of May, Type 45 destroyer HMS *Duncan* was already heading to the Mediterranean and had been earmarked to relieve her sister ship in the Red Sea, when tension rose between Israel and the Lebanese Hezbollah. She was diverted to escort the USS *Wasp* and her amphibious ready group in the eastern Mediterranean. The destroyer would not make it into the Red Sea, and this effectively brought Britain's Red Sea mission to an end.

The forays into the Red Sea by HMS *Diamond* and HMS *Richmond* bought the Royal Navy well and truly into the era of drone and ballistic missile warfare. During the first phase of HMS *Diamond*'s presence in the Red Sea the main threat was aerial drones and when she returned in March the Houthi had progressed to predominately using ballistic anti-ship missiles.

It is testament to HMS *Diamond*'s crew that they were able to successfully engage and destroy a Houthi ballistic missile, despite the ship's radar and weapons not being optimised to engage ballistic threats. The crew repeatedly drilled to detect and engage targets at long range, and they put these skills to use to take on ballistic missiles. A future project known as Sea Viper

ABOVE: The frigate's Sea Ceptor missiles were fired in anger for the first time in March 2024. (MOD CROWN COPYRIGHT)

ABOVE RIGHT: HMS *Diamond*'s Sea Viper missiles are launched from vertical tubes on her foredeck. (MOD CROWN COPYRIGHT)

RIGHT: HMS *Richmond*'s operation room during her engagement on March 9, 2024. (MOD CROWN COPYRIGHT)

ON OPERATIONS

Evolution, is expected to enhance the capabilities of the missile to engage ballistic missile threats at long range but these had yet to be installed on Type 45 destroyers.

During their battles in the Red Sea, the two Royal Navy warships did not engage Houthi robot speed boats that began to be used with increasingly regularity during 2024. The ideal platform to engage these fast-moving craft would have been Royal Navy Leonardo Wildcat HMA2 maritime helicopters armed with Martlet missiles. Up to 16 Marlet missiles can be carried on a Wildcat giving them the ability to engage and defeat swarms of robot speed boats. HMS *Diamond's* Wildcat flew dozens of hours during her patrols in the Red Sea but was not able to engage any surface targets.

While the Royal Navy's duel with the Houthis in the Red Sea has taught it many lessons about modern naval warfare, to date the allied naval operation has yet to bring an end to the rebel group's campaign of harassment against merchant shipping. They proved very adept at hiding their missile and drone launchers for allied aerial surveillance. The US and British government proved unwilling to launch a ground invasion of Yemen to drive the Houthis away from coastal regions to prevent them firing on shipping. The Red Sea campaign appears to be stalemated as *Royal Navy Yearbook* goes to print.

LEFT: HMS *Duncan* was scheduled to replace HMS *Diamond* in the Red Sea in June 2024 but was diverted to the eastern Mediterranean in response to growing tension between Israel and Hezbollah in Lebanon.
(MOD CROWN COPYRIGHT)

BELOW: HMS *Richmond*'s returned home to Plymouth in April 2024 after her successful deployment to the Red Sea.
(MOD CROWN COPYRIGHT)

www.keymilitary.com 21

ON OPERATIONS

Lebanon and Gaza

On Station in the eastern Med

ABOVE: US Army and US Navy technical experts were based on RFA *Cardigan Bay* as they worked to establish the floating harbour off Gaza.
(US Department of Defense)

When war broke out in Gaza in October 2023, British naval forces were swiftly dispatched to the region to help stop the conflict spreading.

With fears growing that British civilians might need to be evacuated from Israel and Lebanon, the amphibious ships of the Royal Navy's Litteral Response Group (South) (LRG(S)), with Royal Marines of 40 Commando embarked were ordered to sail at speed to the eastern Mediterranean.

For three months, the RFA *Lyme Bay* and RFA *Argus* remained on station ready to carry out a non-combatant evacuation operation (NEO) in Lebanon. International diplomacy appeared to contain the crisis, so the LRG(S) was released to continue to proceed into the Indian Ocean and then to Australia for a major exercise.

As the conflict in Gaza raged into 2024, amid growing concern that a famine had taken hold in the war-torn territory, US President Joe Biden ordered the US military to set up a floating harbour moored off Gaza to allow ships carrying humanitarian aid to unload their cargo. Britain offered to help by providing a Bay-class landing ship to act as a logistic base for US soldiers and sailors operating the harbour, known as the Joint Logistics Over-the-Shore (JLOTS) capability.

By early May, RFA *Cardigan Bay* had completed her journey from the Arabian Gulf, where she had been supporting the Royal Navy mine counter measures task force, to the eastern Mediterranean.

During a brief port visit to Cyprus, a company of 80 Royal Marines from 45 Commando embarked on the RFA *Cardigan Bay*. For the next two and half months, the Royal Marines provided force protection for the

RIGHT: RFA *Cardigan Bay* provided key logistic support to the US operation to establish a floating harbour off Gaza to deliver humanitarian aid to starving civilians in the war-torn territory.
(MOD CROWN COPYRIGHT)

ON OPERATIONS

LEFT: A Royal Navy landing craft ferries US Army and US Navy technical experts to and from the US floating harbour. (MOD CROWN COPYRIGHT)

British landing ship and joined with American counterparts to secure the JLOTS harbour.

RFA *Cardigan Bay* was positioned next to the JLOTS harbour, a few miles off the shore near Gaza, to provide accommodation and other support for US personnel involved in loading cargo onto trucks. Landing craft and temporary ferries then shuttled the trucks loaded with humanitarian aid to a temporary pier on the coast at Gaza, where they were driven ashore to be unloaded into aid warehouses.

There was speculation that British personnel would be involved in driving the trucks carrying food and other humanitarian supplies ashore, after President Biden said no GIs would set foot in Gaza because of the risk of them being attacked. British government ministers declined to give specific details of the role to be played by UK personnel. Then Defence Secretary Grant Shapps said in May that the UK would continue to have "a leading role in the delivery of support in coordination with the US and other international allies," without elaborating.

President Biden ordered the JLOTS mission to conclude by the end of July and RFA *Cardigan Bay* was ordered to head back to Britain for a well-earned refit and maintenance period. She was replaced by the RFA *Mounts Bay* in August, and along with 45 Commando, stood ready to carry out a NEO in Lebanon as fighting intensified between Israeli forces and the Lebanese militia group Hezbollah.

The Type 45 destroyer, HMS *Duncan*, sailed to the eastern Mediterranean to provide air defence for the USS *Wasp* amphibious ready group, which was also standing ready in the region to assist with any international evacuation operations from Lebanon.

BELOW: Trucks carrying humanitarian aid were delivered to an improvised landing site on the coast of Gaza by ferries between May and July in 2024. (US CENTCOM)

www.keymilitary.com 23

ON OPERATIONS

On NATO Duty

Steadfast Defender off Norway

As HMS *Prince of Wales* was operating off the United States in late 2024, HMS *Queen Elizabeth* put to sea in European waters to work up her air group ahead of taking part in a major NATO exercise in the spring of 2024. This was to be the largest NATO exercise in several years and was to include an extended naval phase, to test plans to move reinforcements to Europe from across the Atlantic.

The Royal Navy was scheduled to play a leading role in the exercise, including providing an aircraft carrier task group to operate off the coast of northern Norway. In February 2024, HMS *Queen Elizabeth* set sail from Portsmouth to take part in Exercise Steadfast Defender when major faults were discovered in one of her propulsion systems. This resulted in HMS *Prince of Wales* being scrambled from Portsmouth to take her place.

RIGHT: Flying the flag in the Arctic. HMS *Prince of Wales* led the Royal Navy contingent taking part in NATO's Exercise Steadfast Defender.
(MOD CROWN COPYRIGHT)

BELOW: A multi-national NATO task group rehearsed keeping the sea lanes to Europe open during NATO's Exercise Steadfast Defender.
(MOD CROWN COPYRIGHT)

ON OPERATIONS

For a month, HMS *Prince of Wales*, led the NATO Carrier Strike Group, around the icy Norwegian fjords to test alliance naval forces in peer-on-peer conflicts. The aircraft carrier was joined by more than 30 ships, four submarines, and scores of aircraft, along with more than 20,000 personnel from nations including Canada, Denmark, France, and Spain.

The aim of the exercise was to practice projecting naval power into the North Atlantic to keep open lines of communication to Europe in the event of conflict with Russia.

A 100-strong command team from the US Second Fleet deployed to the Norwegian airfield at Bodø, to establish a maritime command element, Commander Task Force North (CTF-N) to control the exercise. The Whidbey Island-class dock landing ship USS *Gunston Hall* sailed to Norway to act as CTF-N's command ship. During the exercise, the British strike carrier HMS *Prince of Wales* and the Italian carrier, ITS *Giuseppe Garibaldi,* worked together in CTF-N. The carrier force sailed off the far north of Norway, practiced carrying out anti-submarine operations and launched simulated strike missions against land targets, before supporting a NATO amphibious task group landing marines on the coast.

HMS *Prince of Wales* was escorted by the Type 23 frigate HMS *Portland* and the fleet tankers, RFA *Tidesurge* and RFA *Tidespring* provided logistic support for British and allied warships. Royal Marine units were landed in north Norway from the RFA *Mounts Bay*.

ABOVE: Exercising under the Northern Lights. HMS *Prince of Wales* operated far north of the Arctic Circle during NATO's Exercise Steadfast Defender. (MOD CROWN COPYRIGHT)

LEFT: RAF F-35B Lightning IIs flew practice strike missions across northern Scandinavia in co-operation with land-based NATO airpower. (MOD CROWN COPYRIGHT)

BELOW: The Fleet tanker RFA *Tidespring* refuelled British and allied warships off the snow-covered coast of northern Norway. (MOD CROWN COPYRIGHT)

ON OPERATIONS

Royal Marines Down Under

400 Commandos Exercise in Outback

ABOVE: Royal Marine ultralight Polaris MRZR-D4 patrol vehicles deployed to Bradshaw Field Training Area in Australia's Northern Territory as part of Exercise Predators Run.
(MOD CROWN COPYRIGHT)

Royal Marines have been training in the outback of Australia's Northern Territory, spearheading a major show of strength with allied forces in the Indo-Pacific region.

More than 400 Royal Marine Commandos deployed for six weeks near Darwin over July and August 2024 for military drills alongside hosts Australia, as well as forces from the United States and the Philippines – aimed at increasing their ability to fight and win together.

Operating 'deep behind enemy lines', the Royal Marines of 40 Commando worked ahead of the main forces in small teams along the vast Indian Ocean coastline and bush land of the Northern Territory, carrying out carefully planned raids on critical infrastructure to pave the way for allies to hit adversary strong points alongside 1 Brigade of the Australian Army.

The British commandos deployed under the cover of darkness by helicopter and raiding craft from the coast, where support ships RFA *Argus* and RFA *Lyme Bay* had been operating as part of a Royal Navy task force – known as Littoral Response Group – South (LRG(S), which is designed to react to world events and crises east of the Suez Canal and into the Indo-Pacific.

RIGHT: During Exercise Predators Run, Royal Marines of 40 Commando carried out live firing drills around Mount Bundey in Australia's Northern Territories.
(MOD CROWN COPYRIGHT)

ON OPERATIONS

Exercise Predators Run explored how the UK's commandos could operate in advance of the main allied force, working far from established supply chains, in small raiding teams designed to cause maximum disruption to the enemy.

Commander of the Land Force of South (LRG(S), Lieutenant Colonel Oliver Denning RM, said: "Exercise Predators Run has presented a fantastic opportunity for us to operate in the Pacific region at a greater scale than we have achieved previously. Working closely with key regional partners and sharing lessons as we learn, it has been impressive to see how quickly we have been able to achieve genuine interoperability between our nations in a short period of time."

RFA *Lyme Bay* and RFA *Argus* were the launch pad for amphibious and helicopter raids, with three AgustaWestland Merlin HC4 aircraft from Yeovilton-based Commando Helicopter Force's 845 Naval Air Squadron flying marines into the action.

Two commando company groups – Charlie and Bravo – of Taunton-based 40 Commando provided the main punch supported by engineers of 24 Commando Regiment Royal Engineers, fire support from 29 Commando Regiment Royal Artillery, logisticians of the Commando Logistic Regiment, together with medics, and reconnaissance specialists from 30 Commando Information Exploitation Group.

"This has been a unique experience," said the officer in charge of Bravo Company, Major Jack South. "It's provided an opportunity to test the limits of our capabilities and push beyond our own boundaries. Treating Exercise Predators Run as a rehearsal for Commando Force operations in a warfighting context has been exceptionally useful. This has been a step change in the way we operate… working in the deep battlespace with disaggregated teams at reach and in highly contested environments."

Together the commandos provided reconnaissance but also struck high-value enemy targets, including command and control nodes and air defence assets, to allow larger follow-on forces to make amphibious landings. The commandos concealed themselves using carefully planned counter surveillance and physical camouflage techniques.

The exercise also included a live firing phase, which saw 8 Battery from 29 Commando Royal Artillery using their L118 105mm Light Guns to support allied forces, while Mortar Troop from 40 Commando formed mixed UK/Australian mortar teams to fire on enemy positions while supported by a Puma drone system to locate targets.

ABOVE: Fire support for British, Australian, Filipino and US forces during Exercise Predators Run was provided by 105mm Light Guns of 29 Commando Regiment Royal Artillery. (MOD CROWN COPYRIGHT)

LEFT: RFA Lyme Bay arrives in Darwin, Australia, to disembark Charlie Company of 40 Commando with a fleet of vehicles ranging from over 40 Polaris MRZR-D4s and seven Viking armoured vehicles ahead of Exercise Predators Run. (MOD CROWN COPYRIGHT)

BELOW: British Royal Marines Commandos with 40 Commando Group were flown into action for Exercise Predator's Run onboard US Marine Corps MV-22B Osprey tiltrotors. (MOD CROWN COPYRIGHT)

ON OPERATIONS

Around the World Tour

Patrol Vessels in Pacific

Sydney's iconic Harbour Bridge and Opera House come into view from HMS *Tamar*, during a visit ahead of an exercise with the Royal Australian Navy to test uncrewed underwater vehicles. (MOD CROWN COPYRIGHT)

RIGHT: Filipino sailors carried out boarding training with the crew of HMS *Spey* during a visit to Manila by the Royal Navy patrol vessel. (MOD CROWN COPYRIGHT)

BELOW: Since 2021 the crew of HMS *Tamar* have seen the sights of the South Pacific during their round the world mission. (MOD CROWN COPYRIGHT)

In September 2021, HMS *Spey* and her sister ship, HMS *Tamar*, departed Portsmouth to be forward deployed to the Indo-Pacific region for a minimum of five years, under the banner Operation Woodwall. The deployment was aimed at establishing a permanent Royal Navy presence in this key region and use it as springboard to set up links and joint training with friends and partners across the Indo-Pacific.

Sustaining the two River-class offshore patrol vessels (OPVs) on the other side of the world is new territory for the modern Royal Navy. Crew switchover takes place every four or five months, to keep personnel fresh and allow them time with their families. Maintenance, including periods in dry docks for repairs in Japan, is also undertaken with local shipyards and navies.

Over the past year the two OPVs have operated in different areas of the region, with HMS *Tamar* working in the South Seas and off Australia and HMS *Spey* sailing in the northwest Pacific and Indian Ocean.

HMS *Tamar* visited the South Pacific Island of Tonga to mark the 65th birthday of King Tupou VI and the 50th anniversary of Tonga's Navy. The latter event prompted ships from across the Pacific to converge in the waters off the capital Nuku'alofa for Tonga International Fleet Review – known in the world of naval acronyms simply as TIFR.

HMS *Tamar* linked up with the USS *Emory S Land* in Cairns, Queensland, to 'plug in' to the US Navy vessel's fuel, water, and power supply. For the first time the Royal Navy made use of the supply chain supporting its French counterpart to deliver ammunition to one of its patrol ships in the Pacific. After considerable planning and a 14,000-mile journey, several thousand rounds of ammunition were handed over to HMS *Tamar* when the ship sailed into the French overseas territory of New Caledonia – midway between Fiji and Australia's Gold Coast.

HMS *Spey* paid a short but extremely fruitful visit to Manila in the Philippines to help promote British industry to the island nation's armed forces. The patrol ship's visit to the Philippines capital coincided with 13 of the UK's leading defence firms such as BAE Systems, Thales, and Leonardo showcasing their equipment and systems to hosts.

ON OPERATIONS

Watching the Gulf

HMS *Lancaster* on Duty

Since 2022, the Type 23 frigate HMS *Lancaster* has been forward deployed in the Middle East to provide a continuous Royal Navy presence in this strategic region.

From its base on the Arabian Gulf Island of Bahrain, HMS *Lancaster* has carried out a variety of missions over the past year, including supporting international naval operations off Yemen, training Kenyan marines, and making port visits to boost links with key allies.

The Royal Navy began forward deploying a frigate in Bahrain in 2019 and HMS *Lancaster* replaced HMS *Montrose* three years later. Under this concept, crews are rotated every four months in Bahrain rather than switching over a complete ship every six months. This saves sailing time and ensures that the forward deployed frigate is always ready for operations in the Middle East.

As well as its frigate, in 2023 and into 2024 the Royal Navy maintained a sizeable presence in the Gulf, including the minehunters HMS *Chiddingfold*, HMS *Middleton*, and HMS *Bangor*, their command/support ship RFA *Cardigan Bay* and the Royal Navy's headquarters east of Suez, the UK Maritime Component Command in Bahrain.

Earlier in 2024, HMS *Lancaster* served two periods of duty with the Combined Task Force (CTF) 150 in the Indian Ocean and Gulf of Aden monitoring suspicious shipping heading to Yemen. This involved the ship making two successful drug seizures in January and April 2024.

HMS *Lancaster* helped bolster security in the southern Indian Ocean as well as strengthening ties with the Seychelles. Her Royal Marine Commandos trained with local forces as part of a UK government £2.5m initiative to deter terrorism, smuggling, trafficking, and piracy in the Indian Ocean. The finale of the visit was a three-day combined jungle workout for *Lancaster*'s Royal Marines detachment with Kenyan marines during a visit to Mombasa.

LEFT: Boarding parties from HMS *Lancaster* have seized illicit arms and drugs from vessels trying to smuggle supplies to the Houthi rebels in Yemen.
(MOD CROWN COPYRIGHT)

LEFT: HMS *Lancaster* has been on patrol on Middle Eastern waters since 2022.
(MOD CROWN COPYRIGHT)

ON OPERATIONS

HMS *Prince of Wales* enters the Drone Era

Aviation Trials on Royal Navy Carrier

ABOVE: HMS *Prince of Wales* large flight deck proved ideal for landing the General Atomics Mojave. This opens the way for future trials on the carrier involving the Royal Air Force General Atomics Protector RG1 drone.
(MOD/CROWNCOPYRIGHT)

Major advances were made in the aviation capabilities of the Royal Navy's Queen Elizabeth-class aircraft carriers in the last half of 2023 following a series of trials with drones and fighter jets armed with heavy bomb loads. These culminated in HMS *Prince of Wales* heading to the east coast of the United States for the final phase of the trials.

Seven years on from HMS *Queen Elizabeth* setting sail for the first time, the Royal Navy is well and truly getting into its stride at generating air groups for its two aircraft carriers.

Both of the carriers are now fully operational and are routinely sailing with their flight decks stacked with Lockheed Martin F-35B Lightning II combat jets and AgustaWestland Merlin HM2 maritime helicopters. A cycle for deployments has been set up, with the carriers taking turns to sail in home waters to qualify new air and deck crews and then sailing further afield as part of a fully formed carrier strike group with a supporting flotilla of warships and supply ships.

In between these 'routine' training cruises, the Royal Navy has been

RIGHT: Deck crews on HMS *Prince of Wales* got hands-on experience of operating large unmanned aerial vehicles during experiments in 2023, including hosting a General Atomics Mojave.
(MOD/CROWNCOPYRIGHT)

ON OPERATIONS

ABOVE: A W Autonomous Systems (WAS) cargo drone landed on **HMS** *Prince of Wales* in September 2023 to kick off a series of experiments with unmanned aerial vehicles. (MOD/CROWNCOPYRIGHT)

keen to use its carriers to take part in force development activities to experiment with new or innovative aircraft and technology.

During the autumn of 2023, HMS *Prince of Wales* was involved in several trials to test operating unmanned air vehicles (UAVs), or drones, from her flight deck. On September 8, 2023, a pilotless aircraft flew on and off a Royal Navy aircraft carrier for the first time. The W Autonomous Systems (WAS) drone flew from the Lizard Peninsula and onto the deck of HMS *Prince of Wales* off the Cornish coast to deliver supplies. An HCMC twin-engine light alloy twin boom drone then flew back ashore in a milestone flight, which pointed the way to the future of naval aviation. It took off from Predannack, the satellite airfield of Royal Naval Air Station (RNAS) Culdrose, and after a flight of about 20 minutes, touched down safely on the deck of HMS *Prince of Wales*.

The intention was to see if it was possible to use drones with a UK Carrier Strike Group in the future to transfer stores and supplies – such as mail or spare parts – between ships, without the need to launch expensive resupply helicopters.

HMS *Prince of Wales* has experimented with drone technology before – notably small quadcopters and Banshee Jet 80+ target drones in 2021- but the trials off the Lizard Peninsula were in a different league, involving a much larger – a ten-metre wingspan and more complex - pilotless aircraft.

These trials were the first stage of a programme during the autumn of 2023 pushing the boundaries of naval aviation. A few weeks later, HMS *Prince of Wales* was cruising off the east coast of the United States and took part in trials with an embarked General Atomics Mojave drone, »

BELOW: A few weeks after the WAS trials, the General Atomics Mojave unmanned aerial vehicle took off and landed from HMS *Prince of Wales* during a cruise off the eastern seaboard of the United States. (MOD/CROWNCOPYRIGHT)

ON OPERATIONS

ABOVE: HMS *Prince of Wales* basked in the Northern Lights off the coast of northern Norway during Exercise Steadfast Defender. (MOD/CROWNCOPYRIGHT)

RIGHT: HMS *Prince of Wales* stood in for HMS *Queen Elizabeth* in Exercise Steadfast Defender in February and March 2024 after a fault was found in the *Queen Elizabeth*'s propeller. (MOD/CROWNCOPYRIGHT)

which is a derivative of the company's larger Reaper and Grey Eagle UAVs. This experimental new American short take-off and landing (STOL) UAV took off and landed for the first time from HMS *Prince of Wales* on November 17.

The Mojave's fuselage is nine metres long, and with a wingspan of 17 metres is six metres wider than a F-35B fighter. The specially modified Mojave was operated remotely by a 'pilot' at a computer terminal and it took-off from and safely landed back on-board HMS *Prince of Wales*.

"The success of this trial heralded a new dawn in how we conduct maritime aviation and is another exciting step in the evolution of the Royal Navy's carrier strike group into a mixed crewed and uncrewed fighting force," said the planner of Mojave's test, Rear Admiral James Parkin, the Royal Navy director of development. "I am delighted that we are taking the lead in such exciting and important work to unlock the longer-term potential of the aircraft carrier and push it deep into the 21st Century as a highly potent striking capability."

The Mojave's test was one of the many trials conducted during HMS *Prince of Wales'* deployment. A plethora of US Marine Corps and Coast Guard aircraft, such as the Lockheed Martin F-35B Lightning II, Boeing MV-22 Osprey, Bell UH-1Y Venom, Sikorsky CH-53E Super Stallion, Bell AH-1Z Viper and Eurocopter MH-65E Dolphin, carried out qualification deck landings on the carrier.

ON OPERATIONS

As well as its experimental work with UAVs and the US military, HMS *Prince of Wales* took part in a series of trials to expand the flight envelope of Britain's main carrier-borne aircraft, the F-35B. This was the third phase of F-35 developmental test (DT-3) flight trials that had started on board HMS *Queen Elizabeth* in 2018. It involved four weeks of flight tests off the eastern seaboard of the United States. These tests were conducted to gather data to expand the flight envelope of the 5th generation jets.

During October and early November 2023, three test pilots flying two specially instrumented F-35B aircraft of the Patuxent River F-35 Integrated Test Force (PAX ITF) performed close to 150 short take-offs (STOs), approximately 80 vertical landings (VLs), and almost 60 shipborne rolling vertical landings (SRVLs), while PAX ITF flight test engineers collected data, and compared it to models, before making initial analyses.

"The last four weeks at sea have been the busiest HMS *Prince of Wales* has ever seen," said Captain Richard Hewitt, the ship's commanding officer. "Watching the F-35B perform the first ever night SRVL was amazing and a real testament to the integration of the F-35 team and my ship's company. The test points achieved will not only improve UK F-35B operations, but those of our F-35B programme partners and allies as well."

"The integration of our teams to realise approximately 150 test points of the F-35B program will potentially increase the way the UK can operate the F-35," said Lieutenant Commander Jamie Elliott, the carrier's air engineering department head. "SRVL, night SRVL, and heavy load (bombs) test points yielded data that will inform any future decisions about the possible F-35B operational clearance to take-off and land heavier, operate in heavier sea states, and turn the jets around faster for more sorties."

ABOVE: Instrumented F-35B aircraft of the Patuxent River F-35 Integrated Test Force were used for the trails on HMS *Prince of Wales*. (MOD/CROWN COPYRIGHT)

BELOW: The flight clearances of UK F-35Bs were expanded during HMS *Prince of Wales'* cruise off the eastern seaboard of the United States. (US NAVY)

TECHNICAL ANSWERS

Propeller Trouble

What is Wrong with Our Carriers?

In February 2024, HMS *Queen Elizabeth* was days away from sailing out of Portsmouth to join Exercise Steadfast Defender off the coast of northern Norway. Rather than take her place in a major NATO exercise, the Royal Navy flagship never got out of her home port after serious technical problems were found with the ship's propeller shaft.

Vice Admiral Andrew Burns, the Royal Navy's fleet commander issued a statement which read: "routine pre-sailing checks yesterday identified an issue with a coupling on HMS *Queen Elizabeth*'s starboard propeller shaft. As such, the ship will not sail on Sunday. HMS *Prince of Wales* will

RIGHT: HMS *Queen Elizabeth* under construction at Rosyth dockyard in Fife. She is the biggest warship ever built for the Royal Navy and incorporated a great deal of new technology.
(MOD CROWN COPYRIGHT)

BELOW: HMS *Prince of Wales* was mobilised at a few days notice in February 2024 to take the place of her sister carrier on a major NATO exercise after she suffered mechanical problems with her propeller shaft.
(MOD CROWN COPYRIGHT)

TECHNICAL ANSWERS

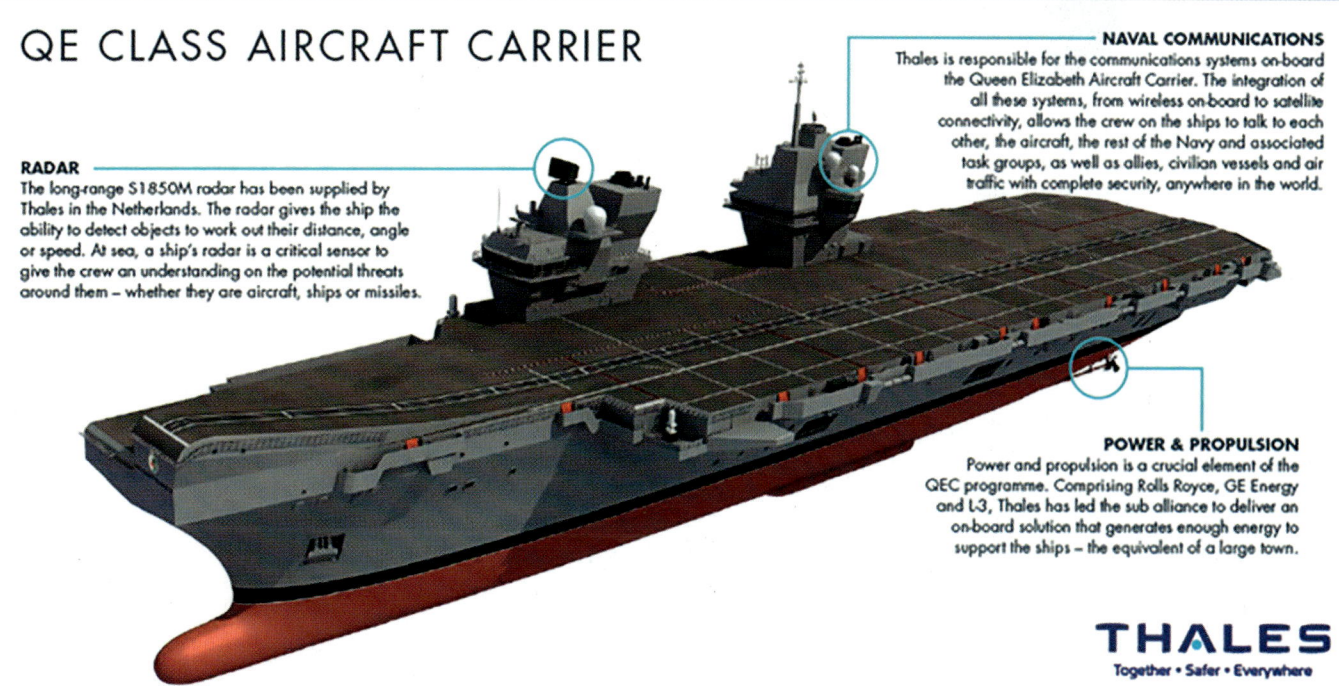

QE CLASS AIRCRAFT CARRIER

RADAR
The long-range S1850M radar has been supplied by Thales in the Netherlands. The radar gives the ship the ability to detect objects to work out their distance, angle or speed. At sea, a ship's radar is a critical sensor to give the crew an understanding on the potential threats around them – whether they are aircraft, ships or missiles.

NAVAL COMMUNICATIONS
Thales is responsible for the communications systems on-board the Queen Elizabeth Aircraft Carrier. The integration of all these systems, from wireless on-board to satellite connectivity, allows the crew on the ships to talk to each other, the aircraft, the rest of the Navy and associated task groups, as well as allies, civilian vessels and air traffic with complete security, anywhere in the world.

POWER & PROPULSION
Power and propulsion is a crucial element of the QEC programme. Comprising Rolls Royce, GE Energy and L-3, Thales has led the sub alliance to deliver an on-board solution that generates enough energy to support the ships – the equivalent of a large town.

THALES
Together • Safer • Everywhere

---

take the place of HMS *Queen Elizabeth* on NATO duties and will set sail for Exercise Steadfast Defender as soon as possible."

A month later, the 65,000-ton aircraft carrier made its way to Rosyth dockyard in Fife on one propeller to undergo five months of major repairs. The incident was deeply embarrassing for the Royal Navy, the Ministry of Defence, and the British shipbuilding industry. British participation in a high-profile NATO exercise was put at risk. When a £3bn warship which is less than a decade old breaks down, it is bound to generate bad media coverage and prompt parliamentarians to ask ministers pointed questions.

What made it worse was that only 18 months earlier, sister ship HMS *Prince of Wales* had suffered an apparently similar problem as she headed to America for a period of flight trials. And this was not long after the *Prince of Wales* had suffered two engine room floods. Britain's aircraft carriers looked jinxed.

If that was not enough, in July 2023 the US military halted all deliveries of Lockheed Martin F-35 Lightning II stealth jets – including those to Britain - because the manufacturer had failed to complete an upgrade successfully. For a year, the stop order was in place, delaying the delivery of Britain's last 13 F-35B jets. This led to more headlines, saying Britain had spent £6bn on aircraft carriers and had not bought enough jets to fill their flight decks.

Britain's pair of Queen Elizabeth-class aircraft carriers have always generated controversy due to their astronomical costs and worries that they were obsolete in the era of 'ship killing' precision guided missiles and drone swarms. The spate of breakdowns added to the concern that Britain's aircraft carriers were white elephants.

So, what is the real problem with Britain's aircraft carriers?

The carriers set sail from Rosyth in 2017 and 2019 respectively and at first their entry to service seemed to go relatively smoothly. HMS *Queen Elizabeth* suffered a pipe leak in July 2019, but it was not considered a major issue. The first hint of more serious trouble was in May 2020 when the engine room of HMS *Prince of Wales* was hit by flooding after a water pipe burst. Then, in October 2020, her fire main failed and several machinery compartments were swamped with several feet of sea water, which caused damage to electrical cables. It took several months to pump out the »

ABOVE: The Queen Elizabeth-class carriers incorporate a great deal of advanced technology to reduce their crew size and enhance aircraft sortie generation. (THALES)

BELOW: After five months in dry dock in Rosyth for repairs, HMS *Queen Elizabeth* sailed under the Forth railway bridge en route to Portsmouth to rejoin the fleet. (MOD CROWN COPYRIGHT)

TECHNICAL ANSWERS

ABOVE: HMS *Queen Elizabeth* returned to Portsmouth during Cowes Week in July 2024.
(MOD CROWN COPYRIGHT)

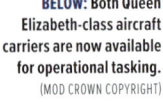

BELOW: Both Queen Elizabeth-class aircraft carriers are now available for operational tasking.
(MOD CROWN COPYRIGHT)

water and repair the damage, at a reported cost of more than £5m. The Royal Navy never fully explained what caused the flooding, but several unofficial sources blamed poor manufacturing of piping joints that were waived through acceptance tests in the haste to make sure the ship did not miss its entry to service date. Leaking pipes on ships are not uncommon and the flooding incidents were not 'showstoppers', according to the Royal Navy.

This all took a more serious turn in August 2022 when HMS *Prince of Wales* was a day out of Portsmouth when her starboard propeller shaft appeared to fail. She had been heading towards the eastern seaboard of the United States to undertake flight trials and host the Atlantic Future Forum trade and economic conference in New York, so this led to red faces across the Royal Navy. Fortunately, HMS *Queen Elizabeth* was available to take on the tasking and had a rapid transit to New York to allow the high-profile event to take place.

HMS *Prince of Wales* headed to the dry dock at Rosyth to be taken out of the water so repairs could be made to her propeller shaft. Subsequent investigations revealed that the ship's unique propulsion system was to blame.

The size of the Queen Elizabeth-class carriers means they cannot be fitted with traditional one-piece propeller shafts. Instead, the shafts are made up of three pieces that are joined together by couplings. They in turn are protected by plastic coverings to stop sea water entering the joints, potentially causing corrosion, and putting the integrity of the whole shaft at risk. One of the couplings on HMS *Prince of Wales* was found to have completely failed.

Rear Admiral Steve Moorhouse, the Royal Navy's director of force generation, confirmed there had been: "significant damage to the shaft and the propeller and some superficial damage to the rudder. There is no damage to the rest of the ship."

After arriving in Rosyth in October 2022, the ship remained

TECHNICAL ANSWERS

HMS *Prince of Wales* undergoes a period of intense maintenance after returning from a deployment. Between cruises the flight deck is routinely checked to make sure the coating that protects the surface from the heat of F-35B jet exhausts has not been damaged. (HASSOCKS5489)

there until the following July to allow both her propeller shafts to be replaced with new ones, which had to be specially made, after sea water corrosion was detected. The plastic coverings had failed to protect the couplings on the starboard shaft. Inspections and analysis revealed that a whole new lubrication system for the coupling's bearings were needed. As a precaution both shafts on the ship were replaced after the new lubrication system was designed.

Fast forward to February 2024 and HMS *Queen Elizabeth* was hit by a very similar problem before she sailed for Exercise Steadfast Defender.

Inspections prior to her sailing had detected some water ingress on HMS *Queen Elizabeth's* shaft couplings but it had initially been hoped that the installation of the new lubrication systems and couplings could be put off, until a major overhaul that was scheduled for 2025. But in the final days before the exercise there were worries that corrosion might suddenly get worse and cause a coupling failure, as was the case on HMS *Prince of Wales*. As a precaution the carrier was stood down and did not head to Norway. Her sister ship was mobilised at a few days notice to join the NATO exercise.

When HMS *Queen Elizabeth* arrived in dry dock in Rosyth in March it had originally been intended only to replace the starboard couplings, but it was later decided to give her the full treatment to both shafts, as was the case with her sister ship.

Royal Navy sources say the experience of finding, diagnosing, and rectifying the faults with the couplings had helped them and their industry partners understand how the new propulsion system operates and is impacted by sea water. They described it as a "learning experience," that is common on any new class of warship. One naval expert commented: "warships don't have prototypes any more – the first of class is often the prototype now."

Hopefully, the teething troubles with the couplings are now well behind the Royal Navy and its aircraft carriers will once again be 'ruling the waves'.

BELOW: The arrival and departures of the two Queen Elizabeth-class aircraft carriers from Portsmouth is now routine and it rarely attracts much attention from other sea goers around the port and naval base. (MOD CROWN COPYRIGHT)

SUBSCRIBE TODAY!

Aviation News is renowned for providing the best coverage of every branch of aviation.

Combat Aircraft Journal is renowned for being America's best-selling military aviation magazine.

/collections/subscriptions

*Free 2nd class P&P on BFPO orders. Overseas charges apply.

ON THIS DAY – 1939

Battle of the River Plate
First Major Naval Action of World War Two

ABOVE: The odyssey of the *Admiral Graf Spee* came to an end in the River Plate estuary after her crew set explosives around the battleship's waterline.
(IMPERIAL WAR MUSEUM)

In the first weeks of World War Two, the German heavy cruiser *Admiral Graf Spee* raged across the South Atlantic attacking allied merchant shipping. Britain eventually mobilised a naval squadron to hunt down the German raider. This culminated in the first naval battle of the war, and it was later immortalised in the 1956 film *The Battle of the River Plate*.

The *Admiral Graf Spee*, commanded by Captain Hans Langsdorff, had sailed from Germany in August 1939, days before the outbreak of World War Two, with orders to head for the South Atlantic to attack allied

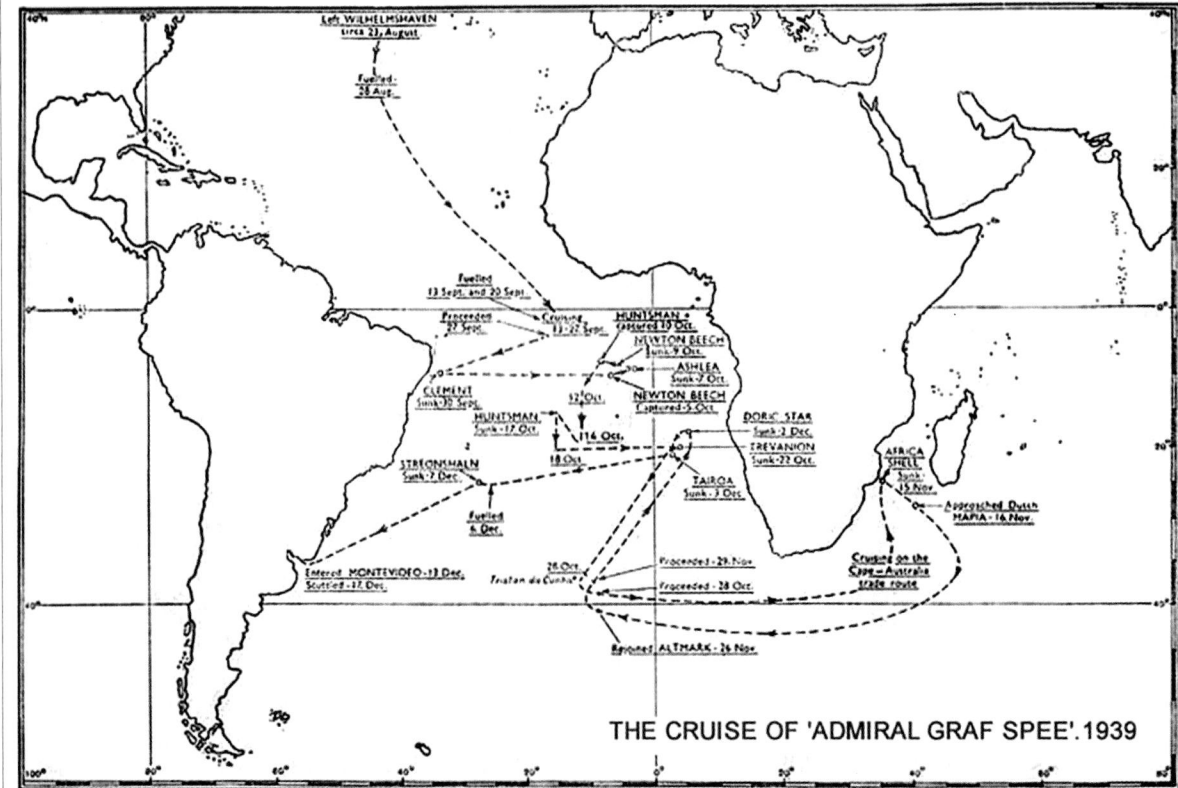

RIGHT: For two months, *Admiral Graf Spee* was hunted around the South Atlantic by the Royal Navy.
(HM STATIONARY OFFICE)

merchant shipping in the southern hemisphere.

Langsdorff received instructions on September 26, 1939, to commence offensive actions and during October and November he sailed his ship around the coast of West and Southern Africa into the Indian Ocean, engaging nine merchant ships. He then turned the *Admiral Graf Spee* around and headed back towards South America.

The Royal Navy mobilised warships to hunt down the German raider and secure its sea lanes to the British Empire. One Royal Navy squadron, commanded by Commodore Henry Harwood and comprising the light cruisers HMS *Ajax*, HMNZS *Achilles*, and the heavy cruiser HMS *Exeter*, finally caught up with the *Admiral Graf Spee* on December 13, 1939.

Harwood's squadron was one of several search groups that had been sent in pursuit by the British Admiralty and they sighted *Admiral Graf Spee* off the estuary of the River Plate near the coasts of Argentina and Uruguay. The *Graf Spee* turned to face her pursuers and Langsdorff hoped her superior firepower would win the day. In the ensuing battle, HMS *Exeter* was severely damaged and forced to retire, making for the Falklands Islands. HMS *Ajax* and HMNZS *Achilles* suffered moderate damage. The German warship appeared to have come off better, but a few British shells found their mark.

It transpired that HMS *Exeter* had dealt a decisive blow. One of her 8in shells had penetrated two decks before exploding in *Admiral Graf Spee's* funnel area, destroying her raw fuel processing system and leaving her with just 16 hours worth of fuel, insufficient to allow her to return home. Langsdorff had little option but to head to safety in the Uruguayan capital, Montevideo, in hope of being able to make repairs in the neutral port.

HMS *Ajax* and HMNZS *Achilles* shadowed the German ship until she entered the port of Montevideo and then patrolled offshore to bottle up their enemy. The British began mobilising warships from around the Atlantic to muster overwhelming force in case the *Admiral Graf Spee* came out to fight. They tried to delay the sailing of the German raider by ordering British merchant ships to sail in and out of Montevideo, as the Hague Convention's neutrality clause prohibited warships from sailing within 24 hours of belligerent merchant vessels.

Langsdorff was receiving intelligence of the gathering Royal Navy force outside of Montevideo and decided he would stand little chance in a stand-up fight with the British. However, the Kriegsmarine high command in Germany told Langsdorff that under no circumstances should he allow his ship to be interned in Uruguay. With the mandated time limit on remaining in Montevideo approaching, Langsdorff set sail on December 17 with a skeleton crew of 40 sailors. A crowd of 20,000 people watched the apparently doomed cruiser heading out into the evening gloom. Once in deep water, Langsdorff ordered the crew to be evacuated onto an Argentine tugboat and minutes later explosives placed around the waterline were detonated. The ship burned for two days before she sank.

Langsdorff and his crew were subsequently allowed to sail to nearby Argentina to be interned for the rest of the war. However, the German captain took his own life on December 19, shooting himself while wearing his full-dress uniform and lying on the *Admiral Graf Spee's* battle ensign. He was buried with full military honours and several Royal Navy officers attended out of respect for his honourable conduct and generous treatment of captured merchant sailors from the vessels he had sunk.

ABOVE: A British-led flotilla including HMNZS *Achilles* gathered off Montevideo to wait for the *Admiral Graf Spee* to emerge and face her pursuers. (IMPERIAL WAR MUSEUM)

LEFT: HMS Exeter suffered moderate damage in the December 13, 1939, engagement with the *Admiral Graf Spee* but the German battleship was critically damaged and had to seek sanctuary in neutral Uruguay. (IMPERIAL WAR MUSEUM)

ON THIS DAY – 1944

The Longest Day

The Royal Navy and D-Day

ABOVE: HMS *Warspite*'s massive guns were brought to bear on the German defences on Sword Beach on the morning of D-Day.
(IMPERIAL WAR MUSEUM)

BELOW: Royal Navy warships protected the invasion force from air, submarine, E-boat, and mine attack as it approached the Normandy coast on D-Day.
(IMPERIAL WAR MUSEUM)

Eighty years ago, on June 5, 1944 thousands of Royal Navy warships and landing craft set sail to Normandy in northern France to deliver more than 130,000 allied troops on the coast of Nazi-occupied Europe.

It was the largest amphibious operation in military history and the naval component of Operation Overlord was masterminded and led by Royal Navy Admiral Bertram Ramsay. Four years earlier he had organised the miracle of Dunkirk to evacuate 338,226 British and allied troops from France at the height of the German blitzkrieg offensive.

In the spring of 1944, Ramsey and his planners had begun to fine tune the details for D-Day, as the landings were code-named. Hundreds of thousands of troops were trained to land on enemy coasts. Overhead, nearly 10,000 allied aircraft protected the skies.

The invasion fleet, which was drawn from eight different navies, comprised 6,939 vessels: 1,213 warships, 4,126 landing craft of various types, 736 ancillary craft, and 864 merchant vessels. The majority of the fleet was supplied by Britain, which provided 892 warships and 3,261 landing craft. In total there were 195,700 naval personnel involved; of these 112,824 were from the Royal Navy with another 25,000 from the Merchant Navy; 52,889 were American; and 4,998 sailors from other allied countries. Marshalling these vessels to land more than 130,000 troops on D-Day was not an easy matter and nothing was left to chance.

Selecting the actual date of the invasion turned on three factors beyond the control of allied planners – tides, availability of moonlight, and the weather. With the best tide and moonlight falling in the first week of June, the allied supreme commander, US Army General Dwight D Eisenhower based his plans on the invasion taking place in this window of opportunity. The invasion fleet needed to sail from ports around Britain, including Scapa Flow in the Orkney Islands in the case of the battleships and cruisers needed to bombard the German defences. These ships needed three or four days to reach their firing positions, so Admiral Ramsay was told to set his fleet in motion on June 1. Allied invasion divisions started moving to their ports of embarkation at the same time to ensure all the vehicles, supplies, and troops could be ready to sail on June 4, so the invasion could take place on the morning of June 5. A bad weather forecast forced Eisenhower to put off the invasion and he only gave the go command in the early hours of June 6. D-Day would now be June 6.

Within two hours of Eisenhower's green light, the naval force set sail and headed for a concentration zone in the centre of the English Channel, dubbed 'Piccadilly Circus'. A fleet of mine sweepers cleared lanes through the minefields to allow landing ships to bring the invasion

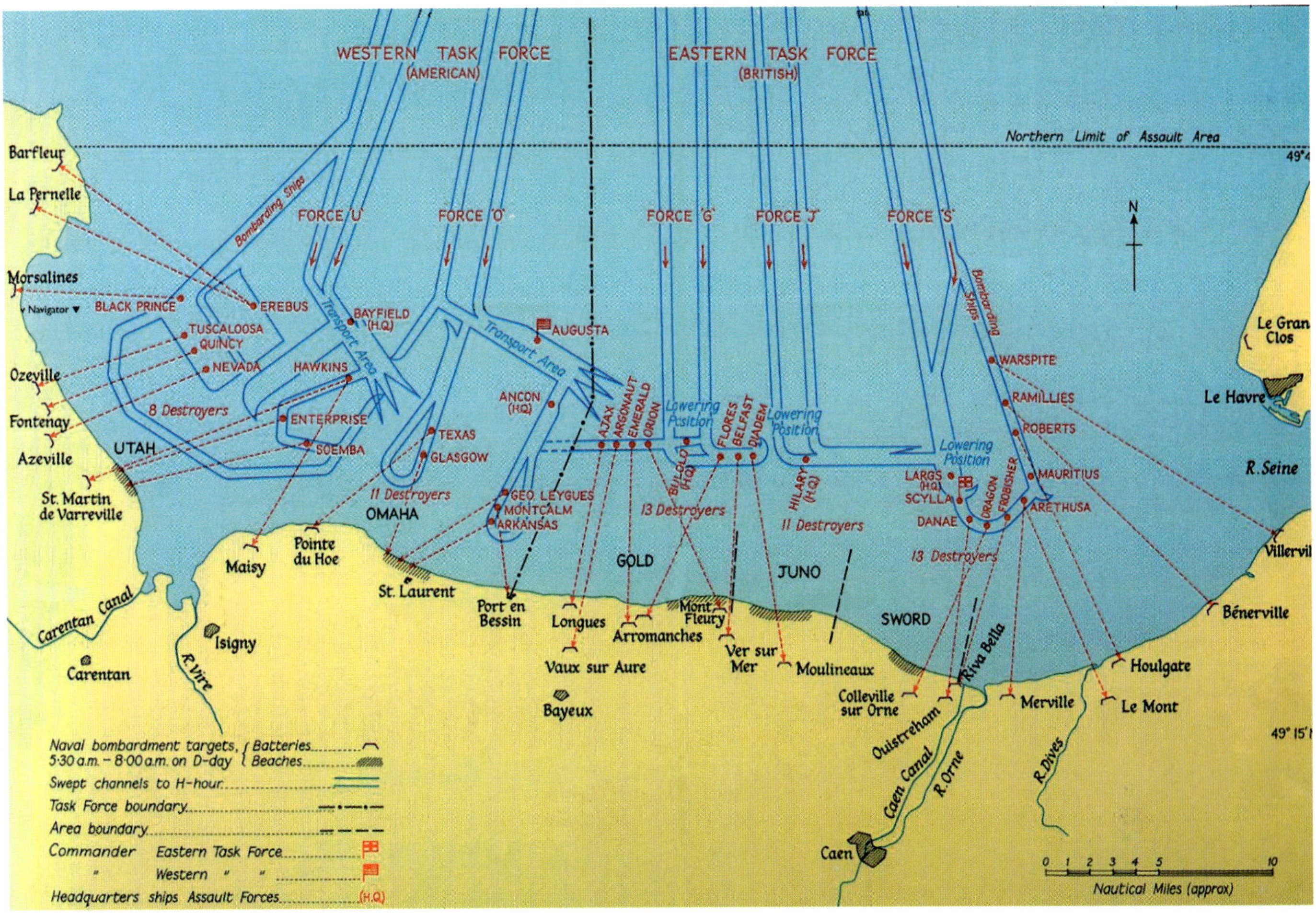

ON THIS DAY – 1944

force to its unloading areas. British mini submarines then marked the route for the landing ships to their dedicated beaches.

By late on the evening of June 5, the first allied warships had arrived off the coast of France and were preparing to open fire. Along the length of the Normandy coast, German troops caught sight of the thousands of allied ships offshore. They did not have long to admire the view before the allied battleships started to blast apart the Atlantic Wall. Soon the landing craft were heading ashore carrying the first wave of assault troops. Despite heavy resistance on some beaches, including Omaha Beach were US troops ran into strong defences, the assault troop were firmly established ashore on the French coast by June 6. D-Day was a success. However, this was not the end of matter for the Royal Navy and its allies at sea. For the next three months, convoys of supply ships were guided to Normandy build up the invasion force so it could take on and defeat the German army in France.

ABOVE: The plan for Operation Neptune was highly complex and had taken months to create and organise.
(IMPERIAL WAR MUSEUM)

BELOW: Royal Navy landing craft crews delivering invasion troops from Britain, Canada, and the United States to the Normandy Beaches.
(IMPERIAL WAR MUSEUM)

BELOW: More than 3,000 Royal Navy landing craft were sent ashore on D-Day.
(IMPERIAL WAR MUSEUM)

ON THIS DAY – 1949

Allied Naval Power

75 Years of the Royal Navy and NATO

ABOVE: Royal Navy mine counter-measures vessels are regularly assigned to work with NATO standing task forces. (NATO)

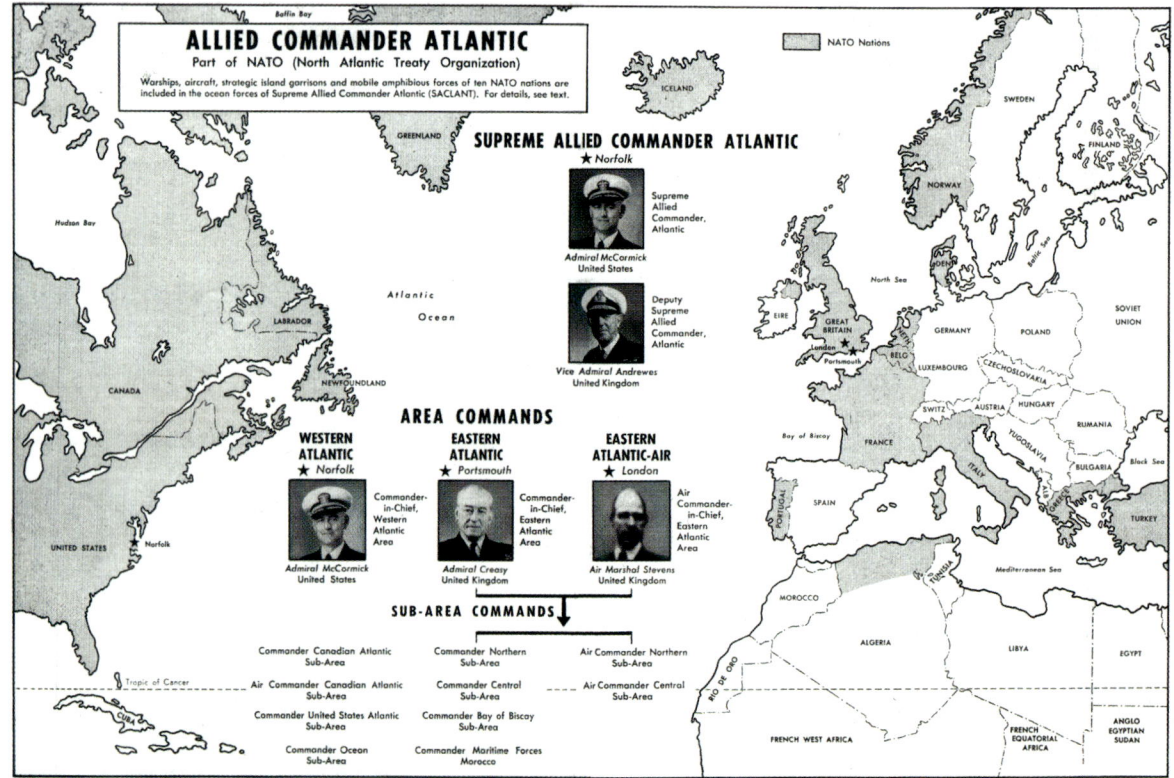

RIGHT: The allied command structure for naval forces in the North Atlantic endured from 1952 through to the end of the Cold War in 1989. (US NAVY)

ON THIS DAY – 1949

LEFT: Royal Navy carrier strike groups regularly supported NATO exercise and deployments from the 1950s to the 1980. (US NAVY)

BELOW: Royal Marine amphibious forces regularly train with NATO allies in northern Norway and the Baltic regions. (MOD CROWN COPYRIGHT)

On April 4, 1949, representatives of 12 nations gathered in the US capital and signed the North Atlantic Treaty. The event set in train 75 years of mutual defence by members of the North Atlantic Treaty Organisation (NATO), to protect their territories from attack.

In July 2024, the heads of government of the now 32 NATO members gathered in Washington DC again to celebrate the anniversary and welcome the alliance's two newest members, Sweden, and Finland, who have joined in the past 18 months.

The Royal Navy has a long history of association with NATO and since 1953 Britain has hosted one the alliance's major naval headquarters at Northwood outside London.

At the heart of NATO is its common military structure that would command allied defensive operations in time of war. In peacetime, these headquarters organise training exercises and prepare contingency plans if war should break out.

Allied naval chiefs' created a unified naval command to cover the North Atlantic region, headquartered in Norfolk, Virginia. Its job in case of war with the Soviet Union was to ensure the sea lines of communications from North America to Europe remained open. A senior US Navy admiral was designated Supreme Allied Command Atlantic or SACLANT. Working for him in Northwood was the British commander of the Eastern Atlantic Area or EASTLANT, who controlled naval operations in Northern European waters. During the Cold War, the commander of the Royal Navy's Home Fleet was dual hatted as the commander of EASTLANT.

Up to the end of the Cold War in 1989, the Royal Navy was focused on supporting EASTLANT's war plans and British warships and the Royal Marines of 3 Commando Brigade routinely took part in NATO exercises. Royal Navy warships were regularly assigned to work in standing naval task groups, operating in peacetime around Europe. These included mine counter-measures groups that were tasked with continuously monitoring the seabed in peacetime to prevent sabotage ahead of any conflict breaking out.

The demise of the Soviet Union in 1991, without a shot being fired led to NATO looking for new roles for its naval forces. British naval forces joined allied sanctions enforcements patrols off the Balkans in the 1990s. The system of standing naval forces continued, but on a smaller scale, and Royal Navy warships took their turn to join them.

The next biggest test of NATO naval power came in 2008 when the alliance launched Operations Allied Provider, Allied Protector and Ocean Shield to protect merchant shipping in the Indian Ocean from attacks by Somali pirates. The Royal Navy joined these missions that successfully neutralised the pirates by 2016.

Since 2012, Northwood has been the headquarters of NATO's Allied Maritime Command, which controls all alliance naval operations in European waters. Headed up by a British vice admiral, NATO's sole maritime headquarters has tactical command on a daily basis of all allied standing forces and maritime security operations in the Mediterranean.

SUBMARINE SERVICE

The Silent Service
The Royal Navy's Underwater Battle Force

Submarines are now at the very heart of Royal Navy operations, hunting down the enemy fleet and providing Britain's nuclear deterrent. In the 1950s, the Royal Navy's senior leadership realised the potential of nuclear power to transform naval warfare, allowing submarines to remain underwater for unlimited periods and move at speed anywhere in the world.

In the final years of the 19th century when other navies were adopting the first operational submarines, the Royal Navy was initially cautious. The then controller of the navy, Admiral Sir Arthur Wilson, famously described submarines as "underhand, unfair and damned un-English" when his staff proposed that the service commission its first underwater vessels.

However, other senior naval officers recognised that submarines could revolutionise naval warfare by allowing surprise strikes to be made against enemy fleets by vessels approaching undetected, underwater. In 1901, the Royal Navy secretly placed an order with Irish-American submarine pioneer John Philip Holland. This submarine became the Royal Navy first functioning submarine, *Holland 1*.

Her keel was laid down February 4, 1901, at the Vickers shipyard in Barrow-in-Furness, which was then in the county of Lancashire. Boundary changes over the generations mean the town is now part of Cumbria. Through the changes the shipyard continued to build submarines, and it is now one of around half a dozen facilities in the world where nuclear powered submarines are designed and built.

RIGHT: HMS *Valiant* was the first wholly British designed and built nuclear powered submarine. She was commissioned in 1966 after being constructed with the first British designed and built nuclear power plant.
(US DEPARTMENT OF DEFENSE)

BELOW: The Astute-class are the Royal Navy's current frontline nuclear powered attack submarines.
(MOD CROWN COPYRIGHT)

SUBMARINE SERVICE

In order to keep the Holland submarine's construction secret, she was assembled in a building labelled 'Yacht Shed'. She was launched on October 2, 1901, and dived for the first time in an enclosed basin on March 20, 1902. Later that year she arrived at Portsmouth, along with the other completed Holland boats and their tender, HMS *Hazard*. The vessels were combined into the First Submarine Flotilla, commanded by Captain Reginald Bacon.

Over the intervening 120 years, the Royal Navy's Submarine Service has grown into one of the world's leading exponents of underwater warfare. In the two world wars, Royal Navy submarine commanders waged aggressive campaigns to sink German and Japanese shipping. At this time, the Submarine Service was nicknamed 'the Trade' and also became known as the 'Silent Service' due to the secrecy surrounding underwater warfare.

In the 1950s, the pace of technological change dramatically accelerated. Using a US-supplied nuclear reactor, construction of the Royal Navy's first nuclear powered submarine, HMS *Dreadnought*, began in 1959. Within months, the first completely British designed and built nuclear powered submarine, HMS *Valiant*, was ordered and she entered service in 1966. Even as construction of HMS *Valiant* was only getting started, the then British Prime Minister Harold Macmillan had decided to move the country's nuclear deterrent from the RAF's V-bombers to nuclear powered submarines fitted with nuclear armed intercontinental ballistic missiles that could be fired from underwater. The change of policy potentially made Britain's nuclear deterrent less vulnerable. The first Resolution-class boat, armed with submarine launched ballistic missiles, was ordered in May 1963 and within five years sailed on her first deterrent patrol. This was a remarkable achievement.

At the same time as the nuclear deterrent submarines, known as 'bombers', were coming into the service, the Royal Navy was also working to accelerate the entry to service of a fleet of attack or 'hunter killer' submarines to take on and defeat the Soviet navy in the North Atlantic. Very soon, a new generation of Royal Navy submarine captains were winning their spurs on dangerous and daring mission into Soviet waters to monitor the Kremlin's fleet.

On May 2, 1982, the Royal Navy made naval history when the Churchill-class boat, HMS *Conqueror*, sank the Argentine cruiser, ARA *General Belgrano*, in the opening days of the Falklands conflict. This was the first and only time a nuclear powered submarine had sunk an enemy warship in time of war. The sinking of the ARA *General Belgrano* was the turning point of the Falklands war, forcing the Argentine navy to return to port and opening the way for successful British amphibious landings to recapture the islands.

The Royal Navy has since continued to invest heavily in nuclear powered submarines and in the 1990s ordered seven Astute-class attack boats at a cost of nearly £10bn.

ABOVE: The Holland-class were the Royal Navy's first operational submarines. (IMPERIAL WAR MUSEUM)

LEFT: Buccaneering Royal Navy submarine crews in World War Two established many of the traditions of the modern Submarine Service, including flying the Jolly Roger after a successful patrol in which enemy ships are sunk. (IMPERIAL WAR MUSEUM)

BELOW: In 1968, Polaris missile armed Resolution-class submarines took over responsibility from the Royal Air Force for providing Britain's nuclear deterrent. (MOD CROWN COPYRIGHT)

SUBMARINE SERVICE

New Dreadnought

Britain's first nuclear-powered Submarine

ABOVE: The Royal Navy entered the nuclear age in 1959 when construction of HMS *Dreadnought* began at Barrow-in-Furness. (MOD CROWN COPYRIGHT)

BELOW: Since HMS *Dreadnought* was built in Barrow-in-Furness, the Cumbrian yard has built boats of every class of British nuclear powered submarine. (MOD CROWN COPYRIGHT)

In 1906 the Royal Navy revolutionised naval warfare by launching its first Dreadnought-class battleship. Fifty years later, the then First Sea Lord, Lord Louis Mountbatten, was determined to take the Royal Navy into the nuclear age.

The United States Navy laid down the world's first nuclear powered submarine, USS *Nautilus*, in 1952 at General Dynamics' Electric Boat Division in Groton, Connecticut. Only three years later she set sail, with the captain sending the historic signal to shore, "Underway on nuclear power."

Lord Mountbatten persuaded the 'father' of the US Navy nuclear submarine fleet, Admiral Hyman G. Rickover, to allow Britain to buy an American nuclear reactor and its associated machinery to kickstart the building of the Royal Navy's first nuclear attack boat, HMS *Dreadnought*. This allowed Vickers Armstrong to lay down the keel of the revolutionary submarine at its Barrow-in-Furness shipyard in June 1959.

In little over 15 months, the submarine was launched and two years later her nuclear reactor was turned on and soon went critical. A few months later she submerged for the first time in the shipyard's Ramsden dock and in April 1963 was commissioned into the Royal Navy, as its first ever nuclear-powered submarine.

Over the next 17 years, HMS *Dreadnought* broke record after record and soon established the Royal Navy as being in the forefront of nuclear submarine operations.

SUBMARINE SERVICE

HMS DREADNOUGHT ATTACK SUBMARINE
Displacement: Submerged: 4,000 tons
Length: 81.0m (265.7ft))
Beam: 9.5m (31.2ft)
Draught: 7.9m (25.9ft 4in)
Propulsion: Single Westinghouse S5W nuclear reactor
Speed: 28kts (52kph; 32mph) submerged
Range/Endurance: Limited only by food and mechanical components
Complement: 113
Armament: Six × 21in (533mm) bow torpedo tubes, 24 rounds carried

During her first years of service, HMS *Dreadnought* took part in many NATO exercises and made port visits around Europe and North America. She also took part in many covert missions to monitor Soviet naval forces around the North Atlantic and Arctic circle.

In September 1967, she left Rosyth naval base in Scotland for Singapore on a sustained high-speed run, which involved sailing 4,640 miles surfaced and 26,545 miles submerged.

Apart from some minor hull-cracking problems, HMS *Dreadnought* proved to be a reliable vessel, popular with her crews. In 1970 she completed a major refit at Rosyth, in the course of which her nuclear core was refuelled and her ballast tank valves were changed to reduce noise.

In early 1971, HMS *Dreadnought* took part in a mission under the Arctic ice cap, codenamed Operation Sniff. On March 3, 1971, she became the first British nuclear submarine to surface at the North Pole. However, on return to Faslane, it was discovered that the ice had caused minor damage to the propeller, bow, and fins.

Dreadnought continued to be used extensively and in 1977 sailed on a covert mission to the South Atlantic to deter an Argentine attack on the Falkland Islands. But by 1980, the boat was showing her age and more capable Churchill-, Valiant- and Swiftsure-class submarines were in service. It was decided to the retire the historic boat and she remains tied up in Rosyth dockyard waiting to be dismantled.

ABOVE: HMS *Dreadnought* was launched in October 1960. (MOD CROWN COPYRIGHT)

LEFT: John Fieldhouse was the second captain of **HMS** *Dreadnought* and later directed the campaign to liberate the Falklands in 1982. (MOD CROWN COPYRIGHT)

LEFT: In 1967, HMS *Dreadnought* made a record breaking run to Singapore to demonstrate the submarine's range and endurance. (ROYAL AUSTRALIAN NAVY)

SUBMARINE SERVICE

Barrow-in-Furness

Home of Britain's Nuclear Submarines

ABOVE: Barrow-in-Furness has been the home to British submarine building for more than 100 years and has been building nuclear submarines since 1959. (BAE SYSTEMS)

RIGHT: The 'A' class submarine was the Royal Navy's first class of British-designed sub. Thirteen submarines of this class were built by Vickers at Barrow-in-Furness between 1902 and 1905. (ROYAL NAVY)

The Cumbrian town of Barrow-in-Furness is home to Britain's only nuclear submarine building yard. At the centre of the Royal Navy's drive to build up its submarine force since the beginning, Britain's first operational underwater vessel, *Holland 1*, was launched from the yard in 1901. The yard built conventional powered submarines in World Wars One and Two and was in at the start of the Royal Navy's nuclear revolution in 1959 when the keel of HMS *Dreadnought* was laid down in the yard.

From 1959 to date, the yard has built 29 of the 32 Royal Navy's nuclear powered submarines – both attack boats and bombers. Three nuclear boats, one Churchill- and two Resolution-class submarines were built at Cammell Laird's yard on the Mersey in the 1960s before a decision was made to concentrate all nuclear submarine work at Barrow-in-Furness.

Six submarines – two Astute-class and four of the new Dreadnought-class boats – are in various stages of construction inside the yard, which is now owned by the defence giant BAE Systems.

The yard has long association with the Vickers company and its successor companies, Vickers Armstrong, and then Vickers Limited Shipbuilding. In 1977, the yard was nationalised for nine years and became part of British Shipbuilders. It was returned to the private sector as Vickers Shipbuilding and Engineering Limited or VSEL. In the 1990s, it was briefly owned by the GEC group before it merged with British Aerospace to create BAE Systems in 1999.

Barrow-made submarines have been in the forefront of submarine development for more than a century and over the past 40 years it has seen a revolution take place in how the yard builds submarines.

In the early 1980s, the Conservative government of Britain's then Prime Minister Margaret Thatcher decided to replace the old Resolution-class submarines armed with Polaris nuclear missiles with new Vanguard-class submarines armed with Trident missiles. The project was of an order of magnitude of complexity that dwarfed the building of the Resolution-class boats. The new submarines displacement was 15,900 tons compared to 8,400 tons of the boats they were to replace.

The US-made Trident missiles to be installed in the new Vanguard-class submarines were also bigger and more complex than their 1960s vintage predecessors.

To deliver the Vanguard-boats, the whole organisation and layout of the Barrow yard had to be transformed. This centred around the Devonshire Dock Hall, or DDH, which was built on Barrow Island in the centre of the shipyard complex. This was Britain's first purpose designed, indoor, submarine assembly facility. Construction between 1982 and 1986 was completed in time for the first Vanguard class boat to be built inside it. HMS *Triumph*, a Trafalgar-class boat was the first submarine to be assembled in the DDH.

The assembly halls are big enough to allow two Vanguard-class submarines to be assembled side-by-side, while parts of a third boat are brought together at the rear of the hall.

A new assembly process was developed for the Vanguard project,

SUBMARINE SERVICE

ABOVE: The Devonshire Dock Hall assembly complex has a submarine lift to lower boats into the water, rather than a traditional slipway. (BAE SYSTEMS)

which saw sections of the submarine being built elsewhere in yard and then moved on giant vehicles into the DDH, where they are welded together. Outside the doors of the DDH is a giant ship lift to lower submarines into the Devonshire Dock for final testing. This replaced the time-honoured tradition of launching submarines down slipways during naming ceremonies. The last Barrow-built boat to be sent down a slipway was HMS *Talent* in 1988.

The ending of the Cold War after the fall of the Berlin Wall in 1989 led to a dramatic scaling back of submarine orders from the Royal Navy. Plans to immediately start building a follow-on to the Trafalgar-class attack boats after the last submarine, HMS *Triumph* was completed in 1991 were put on hold to save money. While work on the Vanguard-boats continued »

LEFT: Hull sections of the new HMS *Dreadnought* are starting to be delivered to the The Devonshire Dock Hall assembly complex. (BAE SYSTEMS)

www.keymilitary.com 51

SUBMARINE SERVICE

RIGHT: Two submarines can be assembled side-by-side inside the Devonshire Dock Hall assembly complex. (BAE SYSTEMS)

BELOW: Residents of Barrow-in-Furness are used to seeing sections of submarine hulls being moved through their streets. (BAE SYSTEMS)

during the 1990s, vital design and development expertise drained away from the shipyard without any replacement work.

In 2001, the contracts to begin work on the new Astute-class attack boats were finally signed and Barrow got back into the submarine building business in earnest. This work got off to a slow start because of the rundown of the shipyard workforce in the previous decade and the Astute-class was beset by delays and cost overruns. The first of class, HMS *Astute* was not launched until 2007 and did not finally enter frontline service with the Royal Navy until 2014.

In 2007, the House of Commons voted to replace the Vanguard-class submarines and preliminary work got underway so that the boats could be replaced at the end of their 25 year-long operational life in the early 2020s. However, after 2010, the then coalition government tried to save money by delaying the start of

SUBMARINE SERVICE

ABOVE: The Devonshire Dock Hall assembly complex provides a purpose-built environment to assemble submarines, uninterrupted by the weather. (BAE SYSTEMS)

building the new Dreadnought class submarines to later in the decade.

Work only really got going in the middle of the 2010s when a £300m extension to the DDH was approved. The new submarines were even bigger than the boats they are to replace, with nearly 17,500-ton planned displacement. As Astute construction started to wind down after the turn of the decade, work gained momentum to completely overhaul the shipyard site. New assembly facilities were built around the site to allow the bigger and more complex hull sections to be pre-assembled, before being moved into the DDH. Work is now well underway on a new HMS *Dreadnought* and when the last two Astute boats are moved out of the DDH over the next 18 months, it will start to take shape inside the assembly hall, ready to enter the Royal Navy around 2030.

The shipyard received another boost in 2021 when Britain signed a deal with the US and Australia to jointly build nuclear powered attack submarines for the Royal Australian Navy (RAN). The AUKUS deal will see BAE Systems team up with US and Australian companies to build new attack boats in Australia.

The new submarine class, dubbed SSN AUKUS, will come online after the last Dreadnought-class is completed late in the 2030s. The first of class will be built in Barrow before the construction of five RAN boats starts in Australia soon after. The SSN AUKUS boats are intended to replace the Astute boats in the late 2030s and early 2040s but the final number has not been confirmed by the Ministry of Defence.

This is intended to ensure that there is not a repeat of the situation in the 1990s when a 'skills gap' was allowed to develop in the Barrow shipyard. In preparation to begin work on the SSN AUKUS, in 2024, BAE Systems announced that it intended to expand its Barrow workforce from the current 12,000 by 5,000 staff over the coming decade. The company also plans to revamp the shipyard to improve production processes, introducting new digital-based design and manufacturing technology, as well as making space for its expanded work force.

The future of submarine building at Barrow-in-Furness now seems secure for another two decades. It looks very likely that the yard will be able to celebrate its 150th anniversary of building submarines for the Royal Navy.

BELOW: HMS *Anson* says goodbye to Barrow-in-Furness and passes Walney Lighthouse to enter the open sea in Morecambe Bay. (BAE SYSTEMS)

www.keymilitary.com 53

SUBMARINE SERVICE

Tomahawk Shooters
Royal Navy Submarine Operations 1990 to 2024

RIGHT: During the 1999 Kosovo war, HMS *Splendid* became the first British submarine to fire Tomahawk cruise missiles in anger. (MOD CROWN COPYRIGHT)

At the height of the Cold War, Royal Navy submarines fought a running duel with their Soviet counterparts under the freezing waters of the North Atlantic. No torpedoes were fired in this stand-off, but rival submarine captains manoeuvred for advantage, hoping to embarrass their opponents and pick up vital intelligence about the capabilities of their submarines.

When the Berlin Wall fell in November 1989, at a stroke the Royal Navy's Submarine Service lost its main opponent. Just as the Ministry of Defence was launching a review to craft a strategy for this new world order, Iraqi troops invaded Kuwait. In January 1991, coalition air power was unleashed on Iraq to open the way for US-led land forces, including a British armoured division, as they advanced to defeat the Iraqi occupation troops in Kuwait.

A major feature of the Operation Desert Storm air war was the first use of precision strike BGM-109 Tomahawk Land Attack Missiles, or TLAMs, fired from US Navy warships and submarines. Nearly 300 missiles hit targets across Iraq with pinpoint accuracy and were even filmed flying down streets in Baghdad by television news crews. News bulletins were also filled with film of downed coalition pilots who had been captured by the Iraqis.

Following the Gulf War, the Royal Navy investigated how it could acquire a precision strike capability to hit targets deep in heavily defended territory, without putting Royal Air Force pilots at risk of death or capture.

The US was approached to sell Tomahawk missiles to Britain to equip Royal Navy Swiftsure- and Trafalgar-class attack submarines. These 'Tomahawk shooters' would give Britain the ability to hit targets more than 1,700km away, within a

BELOW: A Tomahawk cruise missile is test fired from a Trafalgar-class nuclear powered submarine. (MOD CROWN COPYRIGHT)

SUBMARINE SERVICE

few metres' accuracy. This was a revolutionary capability and up until now only the US and the UK have ships or submarines that can fire TLAMs.

In 1995, the US agreed to sell Britain 65 Tomahawks that could be fired through the torpedo-tubes of Royal Navy attack boats. The first missiles were acquired and test-fired in November 1998 from the Swiftsure-class boat, HMS *Splendid*. As well as receiving the missiles and the equipment to load them into its torpedo tubes, the submarine was provided with a specialist satellite communications system to allow it to receive targeting data from allied command posts.

In March 1999, HMS *Splendid* was dispatched to the Mediterranean to join the allied force gathering to join the coming aerial offensive against targets in Serbia in a bid to force it to withdraw its troops from Kosovo. During the three month-long war, the submarine fired 20 Tomahawks. Later in the year a new order was place »

ABOVE: Royal Navy Trafalgar- and Astute-class submarines can all fire the Tomahawk missile. (MOD CROWN COPYRIGHT)

BELOW: The US built Tomahawk cruise missile can hit targets with pinpoint accuracy more than 1,700km from the launch point. (RAYTHEON)

www.keymilitary.com 55

SUBMARINE SERVICE

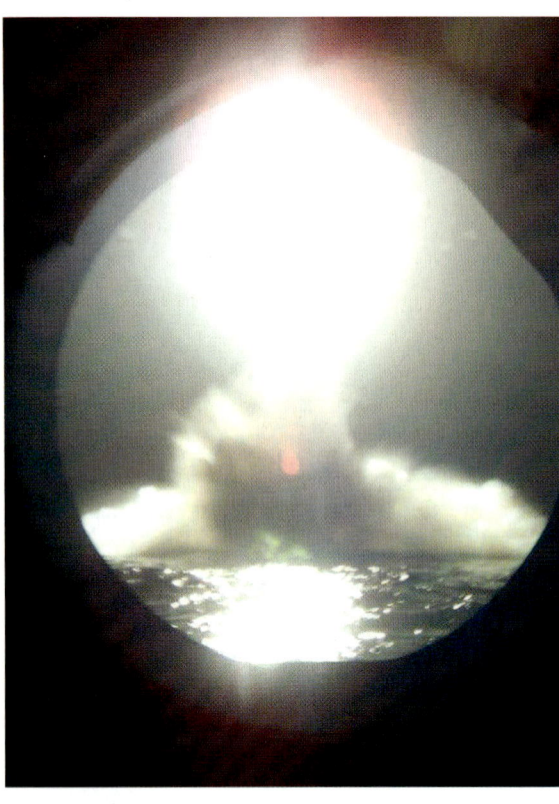

ABOVE: The view from a Royal Navy submarine periscope of a Tomahawk missile being launched at a target in Iraq in March 2003.
(MOD CROWN COPYRIGHT)

BELOW: Inside the control of a Trafalgar-class submarine as it launches missiles during the 2003 Iraq war.
(MOD CROWN COPYRIGHT)

for 20 TLAMs to replenish the Royal Navy's stocks.

Two years later, the Royal Navy's 'Tomahawk shooters' were in action again when Britain sent HMS *Trafalgar* and HMS *Triumph* to join the US-led invasion of Afghanistan in response to the 9/11 attacks on New York and Washington by Osama bin Laden's al-Qaeda network.

Under the banner of Operation Veritas, the submarines fired TLAMs at targets in Afghanistan. Confirmation of their role in the conflict emerged when they returned to their home ports flying the Jolly Roger flag, the Submarine Service's traditional way of denoting a boat had fired live weapons in anger.

When Britain decided to join the US invasion of Iraq in March 2003 it came as no surprise that the Royal Navy's 'Tomahawk shooters' had a key role to play to hit heavily protected targets around Baghdad.

HMS *Splendid* and HMS *Turbulent* were the designated boats for Operation Telic and they were on station in the Arabian Gulf in the days before the war started. Again, both boats returned home flying Jolly Rogers. HMS *Turbulent* is reported to have fired 30 TLAMs during the conflict.

When Britain joined the international intervention in Libya in 2011, HMS *Triumph* was dispatched to the Mediterranean for Operation Ellamy. The submarine was in action during the opening hours of the operation on March 19, joining a barrage with the US Navy to hit key air defence and command port targets. She was in action again on March 20 and 24, hit more air defence targets and Colonel Gaddafi's presidential compound in the capital Tripoli. HMS *Triumph* returned to Devonport in April 2011 flying a Jolly Roger adorned with six small Tomahawk 'axes' to indicate the missile firings.

HMS *Turbulent* was relieved by HMS *Triumph* off Libya, but she returned later to fire more missiles during Operation Ellamy. In total, HMS *Triumph* fired 15 TLAM during the campaign.

These operations showed the capability of the Royal Navy to join in strategic strike campaigns alongside the US Navy and allied air forces. Although the Royal Navy and Ministry of Defence continue to cloak the deployments of 'Tomahawk shooters' in great secrecy, reports have emerged indicating they have been moved into place in several recent crises across the Middle East to give British political decision makers multiple strike options.

In 2013, when tension was mounting over Syrian use of chemical weapons, British TLAM submarines were moved into range to join a US-led strike on the country. In the end intervention was called off. Later in the decade, clashes between the US and Iran also saw British and US 'Tomahawk shooters' moved into range, but diplomacy prevailed, and again, they were not needed.

The Tomahawk-shooting submarines are a prized capability, and the Ministry of Defence

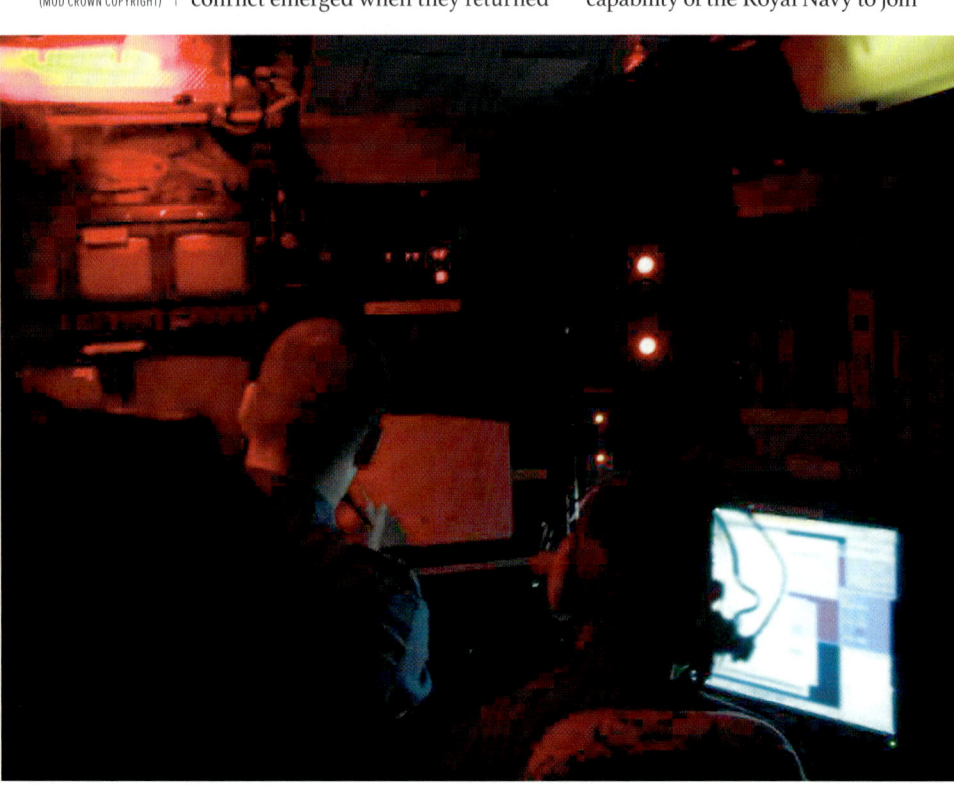

has invested in new and improved versions of the TLAM. In 2004, 64 Block IV TLAMs were ordered, which featured the ability to re-direct the missiles in flight. They entered service in 2008 and six years later 65 more of the missiles were ordered at a cost of $140m.

In June 2022, the UK announced it would be upgrading its Tomahawk missiles again to Block V standard through a £265m contract with the US government. The missiles will be upgraded from 2024. These are an improved version of the Block IV, which feature modernised in-flight communication and target selection.

In the early days of the Tomahawk programme only a handful of submarines could fire the missiles. Eventually all the Trafalgar-class submarines were converted to fire the missiles. As the new Astute-class submarines started to enter service from 2014, they too were all equipped to fire TLAMs as standard. The 'TLAM shooter' is here to stay.

BELOW: The Royal Navy tries to keep a Tomahawk-armed Astute-class submarine in the Mediterranean, ready to respond to any unexpected crisis in the Middle East.
(MOD CROWN COPYRIGHT)

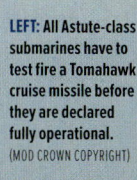

LEFT: All Astute-class submarines have to test fire a Tomahawk cruise missile before they are declared fully operational.
(MOD CROWN COPYRIGHT)

SUBMARINE SERVICE

Britain's New Nuclear Deterrent

The new HMS *Dreadnought*

Britain's next class of nuclear powered submarine is now taking shape in Barrow-in-Furness as part of a 'national endeavour' effort to replace the existing Vanguard-class deterrent boats.

Extending the life of Britain's 'continuous at sea deterrence' into the latter half of the 21st century does not come cheap, and the cost of the project is currently reported to be £30bn. The old 'V-boats' are scheduled to begin retiring early in the 2030s after four decades carrying out Operation Relentless, the UK's strategic deterrence mission.

The aim is to build four new Dreadnought-class submarines, each the length of three Olympic swimming pools, with the first one ready to sail on its first patrol in the early 2030s. At 17,200 tons they will be the largest submarines ever operated by the Royal Navy and one of the most complex machines ever built. Each boat will contain 26.4 miles of pipework and more than 20,000 cables stretching 215 miles – further than travelling between London and Leeds.

Each Dreadnought-class submarine will accommodate 130 crew members, including three chefs and one doctor. For the first time on a British submarine, they will also feature separate female crew quarters, toilets, and washing facilities.

Like the Vanguard-class submarines that they will be replacing in the Royal Navy's Submarine Service, the new Dreadnought-class submarines will be capable of launching US-made Trident II D5 inter-continental ballistic missiles. As part of the renewal of Britain's nuclear deterrent, a new nuclear warhead is being developed by the Atomic Weapons Establishment at Aldermaston in Berkshire. These will replace the existing British warheads that are

BELOW: The new HMS *Dreadnought* will be Britain's biggest every submarine with a displacement of more than 17,000 tons.
(BAE SYSTEMS)

fitted to the Trident missiles used in Royal Navy submarines.

The new submarines will each have three missile compartments, and each compartment will comprise four missile tubes, known as a 'Quad Pack', for a total of 12 missiles, and five deck levels. Dreadnought-class submarines are also to have four 533mm torpedo tubes for Spearfish heavyweight, medium-range torpedoes to provide them with a powerful self-defence capability.

A more effective nuclear propulsion system known as the Pressurised Water Reactor 3, or PWR3, has been designed and built by Rolls-Royce at its Derby site. The new design of the PWR3 leverages technology to deliver key benefits such as simplified operations, a longer service life, and reduced maintenance costs over the lifecycle of the boats.

New innovations in design will make Dreadnought boats even stealthier and they will be the first British submarines to feature X-rudders. Previous Royal Navy submarine designs used traditional rudders, but the new X-rudders will allow the new boats to go faster and operate at greater depth, offering improvements in control and safety. These new rudders will sit in front of the very latest pump jet propulsor, which are designed to reduce the noise of the submarines, particularly at high speeds. The pump jet used in the Dreadnought-class is the quietest yet used on a Royal Navy submarine.

The Dreadnought Programme is described by the British government as an 'incredible national endeavour' that will eventually result in four new submarines being built. HMS *Dreadnought* is the lead boat, and she will be followed by HMS *Warspite* and HMS *Valiant*, which are already under construction at BAE Systems Barrow-in-Furness yard. Boat number four, HMS *King George VI* is at a very early stage of construction.

All the submarines will be assembled under cover in the Devonshire Dock Hall (DDH) complex, which is 260 metres long, 58 metres wide and 51 metres high, making it almost large enough to accommodate the ill-fated Atlantic cruise liner, RMS *Titanic*. The final two Astute-class submarines, HMS *Agamemnon,* and HMS *Agincourt*, are in the later stages of construction in the DDH, and work is moving at a pace to accelerate Dreadnought-class assembly once they are finished.

The new submarines are being built in 16 units, grouped into three 'mega units', known as aft, mid, and forward, in order to optimise the overall build timeframe.

The build phase for all four submarines will take approximately 20 years, which will stretch out into the late 2030s.

The Dreadnought programme supports around 30,000 jobs across »

LEFT: The new Dreadnought-class will continue to be armed with the Trident D-5 submarine launched intercontinental nuclear armed missiles, that currently equip the Royal Navy's Vanguard-class boats. (MOD CROWN COPYRIGHT)

BELOW: Advanced manufacturing techniques are being used in Barrow-in-Furness to build the Dreadnought-class submarines. (BAE SYSTEMS)

VANGUARD-CLASS BALLISTIC MISSILE FIRING SUBMARINES

Displacement:	Submerged: 17,200 tons
Length:	153.6m (504ft)
Beam:	12.8m (42ft)
Draught:	12m (39ft 4in)
Propulsion:	One Rolls-Royce PWR3 nuclear reactor
Speed:	Over 28kts (52kph; 32mph), submerged
Range/Endurance:	Limited only by food and mechanical components
Complement:	130
Armament:	
Four × 21in (533mm) torpedo tubes for Spearfish heavyweight torpedoes	
14 × ballistic missile tubes for 8–12 Lockheed Trident II D5 SLBMs (carrying up to 8 warheads each)	

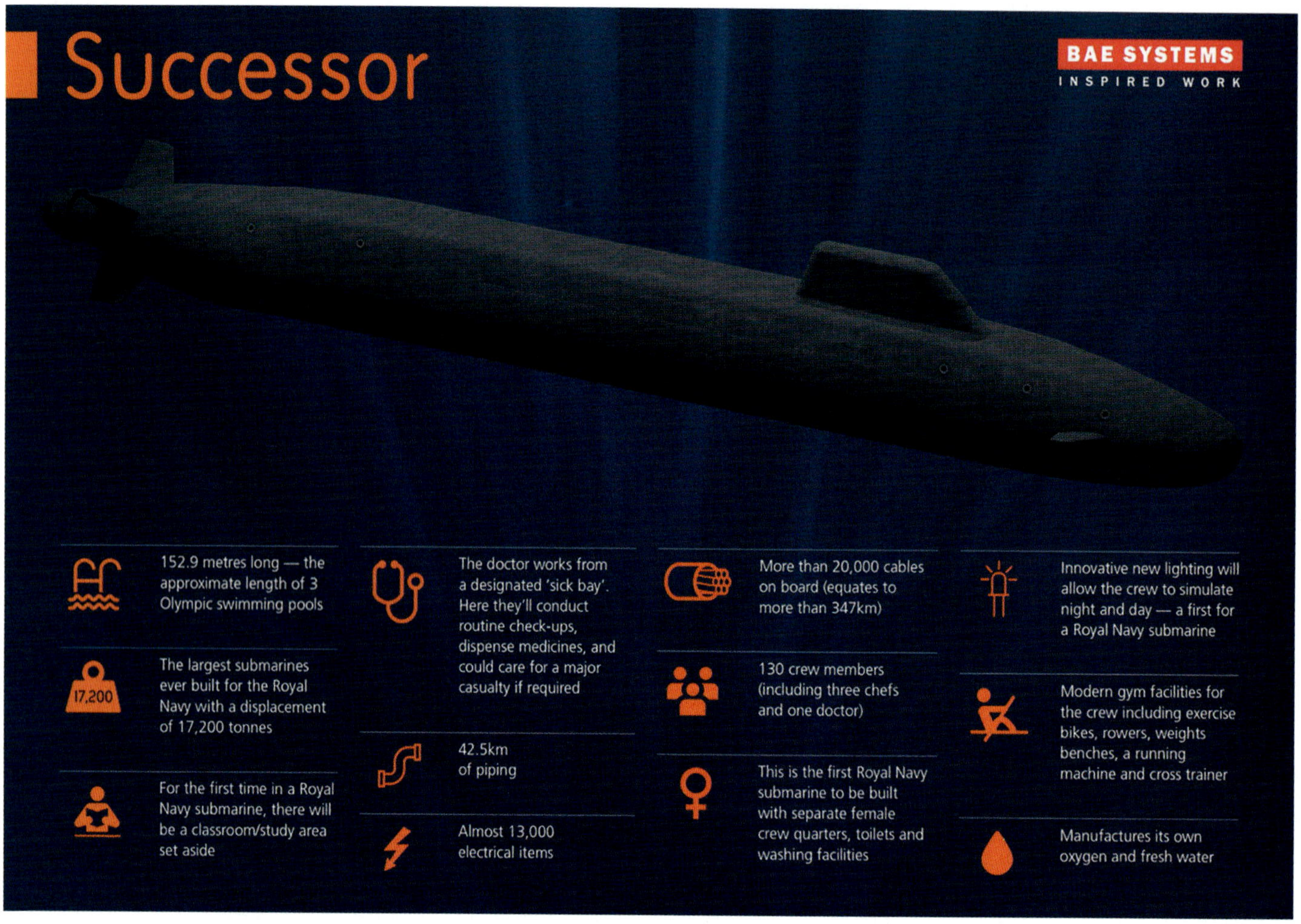

SUBMARINE SERVICE

Successor

BAE SYSTEMS
INSPIRED WORK

- 152.9 metres long — the approximate length of 3 Olympic swimming pools
- The largest submarines ever built for the Royal Navy with a displacement of 17,200 tonnes
- For the first time in a Royal Navy submarine, there will be a classroom/study area set aside
- The doctor works from a designated 'sick bay'. Here they'll conduct routine check-ups, dispense medicines, and could care for a major casualty if required
- 42.5km of piping
- Almost 13,000 electrical items
- More than 20,000 cables on board (equates to more than 347km)
- 130 crew members (including three chefs and one doctor)
- This is the first Royal Navy submarine to be built with separate female crew quarters, toilets and washing facilities
- Innovative new lighting will allow the crew to simulate night and day — a first for a Royal Navy submarine
- Modern gym facilities for the crew including exercise bikes, rowers, weights benches, a running machine and cross trainer
- Manufactures its own oxygen and fresh water

ABOVE: The Dreadnought-class were initially known as the 'Successor' to signify their role to replace the Vanguard submarines. (BAE SYSTEMS)

HMS *DREADNOUGHT* – A LONG TRADITION

At least 11 warships and one submarine of the Royal Navy have borne the name HMS *Dreadnought* in the expectation that they would 'dread nought', or 'fear nothing'.

The first recorded HMS *Dreadnought* was launched in 1553, but the most famous bearer of the name is the 1906 ship, which revolutionised battleship design, making all other warships of the era obsolete because of her 21in gun turrets and high speed. Battleships built after her were referred to as 'Dreadnoughts', and earlier battleships became known as 'pre-Dreadnoughts'. In 1959, the Royal Navy made another major technological leap when it started work on its first nuclear-powered submarine, and to mark the significance, it was also named HMS *Dreadnought*.

RIGHT: In 1906, the new HMS *Dreadnought* transformed naval warfare thanks to her unprecedented firepower and speed. (IMPERIAL WAR MUSEUM)

Britain, from design through to build. It draws on cutting edge capabilities, innovation, and collaboration of the best design and engineering skills available in the country.

The project has been a long time in the making with the work beginning on the concept phase of the 'Successor' programme in March 2007, after an agreement in the House of Commons on the general principle of whether the UK should retain a strategic nuclear deterrent beyond the life of the current system. Nine years later, Parliament again approved the decision to maintain the UK's nuclear deterrent beyond the early 2030s and the programme moved into its manufacturing phase.

Construction of the first submarine began with the cutting of the steel in October 2016. The Dreadnought Alliance was formed when the Ministry of Defence established a new agreement with its two key industrial partners on the Dreadnought programme: BAE Systems and Rolls-Royce. The ministry then formed its own Submarine Delivery Agency to oversee the industry partners in the alliance.

Work then accelerated and in November 2022, the first pressure hull for Dreadnought Boat 1 moved into the DDH complex. A year later the largest segment, or 'mega unit', of HMS *Dreadnought* to be completed so far was moved into the DDH.

It is also the longest section of a submarine moved through the streets of Barrow-in-Furness from BAE Systems' fabrication facility to the cavernous DDH which dominates the skyline of the Cumbrian town. At over 20 metres in length, it is the longest submarine unit to move by road since the fore-end mega-unit moved to the DDH for the final Vanguard boat in the mid-1990s. It was protected against the elements by what must be the world's largest black bin bag.

With HMS *Dreadnought* now taking shape inside the DDH, the long work on the project to replace Britain's nuclear deterrent submarines is starting to come to fruition. However, there is still a long way to go until HMS *Dreadnought* sails from Faslane on her first 'continuous at sea deterrence' patrol.

ABOVE: HMS *Dreadnought* is expected to enter service at the end of this decade. (BAE SYSTEMS)

BELOW: Hull sections of HMS *Dreadnought* are already being delivered to the Devonshire Dock Hall submarine assembly complex. (BAE SYSTEMS)

THE FLEET TODAY

Britain's Naval Power
The Royal Navy Fleet in 2024

RIGHT: Six Type 45 destroyers provide air defence of the fleet.
(MOD CROWN COPYRIGHT)

In 2024 the Royal Navy boasts the largest naval fleet in Europe and is a major global maritime power.

It currently numbers four ballistic missile firing submarines, six nuclear-powered attack submarines, two 65,000-ton aircraft carriers, 15 frigates and destroyers, five amphibious landing ships, seven mine counter-measures vessels and five logistic support ships. A fleet of 34 fighter jets and more than 80 helicopters are available to be embarked on Royal Navy warships. Just under 6,000 Royal Marines are held at high readiness to work with the fleet around the world.

The Royal Navy bases its warships, submarines, and support vessels at three main naval bases in Britain. Portsmouth is home to the aircraft carriers and destroyers; Devonport in Plymouth is the home port of the majority of the frigate force and the amphibious shipping, with the bulk of the Royal Marines Commando Force based in or near the city. And Faslane naval base in the Clyde, Scotland is home to the nuclear submarine force and many mine counter-measure vessels.

The helicopters of the Fleet Air Arm are based at RNAS Culdrose in Cornwall and RNAS Yeovilton in Somerset. There is also a growing Royal Navy presence at RAF Marham in Norfolk, where the Lockheed Martin F-35B Lightning II jump

BELOW: The Royal Navy's four Vanguard-class submarines provide Britain's nuclear deterrent.
(MOD CROWN COPYRIGHT)

THE FLEET TODAY

ABOVE: Royal Navy warships and support ships joined NATO's Exercise Steadfast Defender off Norway in February and March 2024. (MOD CROWN COPYRIGHT)

jets are based when they are not embarked on the Queen Elizabeth-class aircraft carriers.

To support its global mission, the Royal Navy has established a network of bases and facilities in British Overseas Territories and in allied countries. Thanks to its strong links to the United States Navy, British warships and submarines can also routinely make use of American naval bases. Partnerships with the US Navy are essential to maintaining the operational effectiveness of the Royal Navy's submarine force, including overhauling Britain's Trident D-5 missiles at the King's Bay naval base in Georgia and carrying out live missile and torpedo firing at the Atlantic Undersea Test and Evaluation Center (AUTEC), off the Bahamas.

The historic naval base on Gibraltar is increasingly being used as a hub to support operations in the Mediterranean, Caribbean, off West Africa and in the South Atlantic. HMS *Jufair* on the island of Bahrain in the Arabian Gulf is the United Kingdom Naval Support Facility in the Middle East.

The British government has signed an agreement with Oman to allow access to its port at Duqm, which has dry docks capable of repairing Queen Elizabeth-class aircraft carriers. And, to support Royal Navy operations in the Far East, agreements have been made with several countries in the region to gain access to their ports and naval bases. A refuelling and resupply facility has also been opened on the island of Singapore. Additionally, the Royal Navy has repaired and supported its River-class patrol vessels in Australia and Japan.

Under the AUKUS deal with Australia and the United States, the Royal Navy's presence in the Indo-Pacific region will be boosted when Astute-class nuclear attack submarines will temporarily be based in near Perth in Western Australia from 2027.

BELOW: HMS *Prince of Wales* is working up to lead a Royal Navy carrier strike group to the Far East in 2025. (MOD CROWN COPYRIGHT)

THE FLEET TODAY

Submarine Force
Bombers and Attack Boats

HMS *Vanguard* returned to the fleet in 2023 after a seven-year-long refit and refuelling period in Devonport dockyard. This year the submarine has been undergoing work-up training before returning to take her place in the continuous at sea deterrent cycle of patrols. The submarine made the headlines in February 2024 when it was reported that a missile firing on a test range off the coast of the United States suffered a malfunction, when its second stage boosters failed to ignite. The Ministry of Defence said the test was a success, despite the incident, commenting, "the anomaly was event specific, and therefore there are no implications for the reliability of the wider Trident missile systems and stockpile." (MOD CROWN COPYRIGHT)

HMS *Victorious* arrived in Devonport dockyard in May 2023 to begin a deep maintenance period, which is expected to last three or four years. Once completed, this will allow the boat to remain on continuous at sea deterrent duty until well into the 2030s, when the first Dreadnought-class boats should be coming into service. According to the Ministry of Defence, the refit is expected to cost £560m.

The submarine was withdrawn from duty in 2022 but delays in the refitting and refuelling of HMS *Vanguard* meant she had to spend several months alongside at Faslane naval base until a dry dock became available in Devonport. Her fragile material state was highlighted in December 2022 when she had to surface after a fire. The boat had been returning to Faslane after unloading her Trident missiles for maintenance at the King's Bay naval base in Georgia. (MOD CROWN COPYRIGHT)

THE FLEET TODAY

The third submarine in the Vanguard-class, HMS *Vigilant*, has been the mainstay of the Royal Navy's continuous at sea deterrent operations for most of this decade. After HMS *Vanguard* and then HMS *Victorious* were taken out of action for refits and refuels it fell to HMS *Vigilant* and HMS *Vengeance* to take up the slack.

The submarine underwent a refit and refuelling between 2009 and 2012, so she is not expected to require a major maintenance period until she is retired around the turn of the decade. From her home base at Faslane on the Clyde, HMS *Vigilant* carries out deterrent patrols in the North Atlantic region. During these patrols, the Royal Navy's Vanguard-class submarines remain submerged and avoid being detected by adversary naval forces. (MOD CROWN COPYRIGHT)

The fourth boat in Vanguard-class entered Royal Navy service in 1999. She underwent a major refuel and refit between 2012 and 2015 so is expected to remain in service into the 2030s, when the replacement Dreadnought-class boats are due to enter service.

HMS *Vengeance* had to step up its operations to fill the gap in continuous at sea deterrent coverage caused by the heavy maintenance requirements of HMS *Vanguard* and then HMS *Victorious*. This came peaked in August 2023 when she sailed on patrol that eventually lasted 201 days.

The seven-month long patrol was only six days short of the record of 207 days, set in 2001 by HMS *Victorious*. This was part of a growing trend in increasing days at sea for the Vanguard-class boats this decade that has seen patrol lengths averaging at around 160 days, or five months. (MOD CROWN COPYRIGHT)

VANGUARD-CLASS BALLISTIC MISSILE FIRING SUBMARINES

Displacement: Submerged: 15,900 tons

Length: 149.9m (491ft 10in)

Beam: 12.8m (42ft)

Draught: 12m (39ft 4in)

Propulsion: Single Rolls-Royce PWR2 nuclear reactor

Speed: Over 25kts (46kph; 29mph), submerged

Range/Endurance: Limited only by food supplies and mechanical components

Complement: 135

Armament:

Four × 21in (533mm) torpedo tubes for Spearfish heavyweight torpedoes

16 × ballistic missile tubes for: 8–16_Lockheed Trident II D5 SLBMs (carrying up to 8 warheads each)

THE FLEET TODAY

HMS *Triumph* is the last of the Trafalgar-class nuclear-powered attack submarines to remain in Royal Navy service.

After being commissioned in 1991, the submarine has had an eventful operational career, including firing Tomahawk land attack missiles at targets in Afghanistan in 2001 and Libya in 2011.

The boat returned to sea in December 2022 after a four-year-long major refit period and this is expected to allow her to remain in operational service into 2025. It had previously been announced that she would be retired by the end of 2024 but maintenance issues with the Astute-class and heavy operational demands means the boat is needed in the fleet.

The submarine was photographed in the Gibraltar naval base in June 2024, suggesting she was carrying out operations or exercises in the Mediterranean region. (MOD CROWN COPYRIGHT)

As the first of class, HMS *Astute* blazed a trail for the Royal Navy's newest class of nuclear powered attack submarines. She achieved many firsts, including launching of the Tomahawk land attack missiles in 2011 and sailed to South Korea and Japan in 2021 as part of the Carrier Strike Group 2021 deployment.

However, HMS *Astute* has also been plagued by bad luck. Her first captain was sacked after she ran aground off the Isle of Skye in 2010. A naval officer was killed, and another injured in 2011 after a drunken sailor went on a shooting spree onboard the boat. The boat also suffered numerous technical issues in the years after being formally commissioned into the fleet in 2010, so did not undertake an operational patrol until 2014.

The submarine was very active in 2023 but since the start of 2024 has been alongside at the Faslane naval base undergoing maintenance. (BAE SYSTEMS)

HMS *Anson* is the latest nuclear-powered attack submarine to enter Royal Navy service after being formally commissioned into the fleet in August 2022. Unusually, this took place within the Devonshire Hall Dock basin in Barrow-in-Furness and the submarine did not sail from the BAE Systems' shipyard in Cumbria for Faslane naval base until February 2023 to begin her sea trials.

The submarine's crew then carried out work up training and more sea trials before heading to the Atlantic Undersea Test and Evaluation Centre (AUTEC) off the Bahamas in early 2024. During her time at AUTEC, HMS *Anson* carried out successful test-firings of Spearfish homing torpedoes and Tomahawk land attack missiles. After completing these firings, the submarine returned to Faslane in April 2024 but has not been to sea since then to allow maintenance to be undertaken. (MOD CROWN COPYRIGHT)

THE FLEET TODAY

HMS *Artful* has been operational with the fleet since 2016 and has seen extended operational deployments. In the summer of 2021, *Artful* supported the Carrier Strike Group 2021 deployment and took part in exercises in the Indian Ocean region, with US Navy, Dutch, and Indian naval forces. For 15 months, HMS *Artful* has been alongside at Faslane undergoing maintenance. (BAE SYSTEMS)

The second boat in the Astute-class was commissioned into the fleet in 2013 and soon afterwards successfully fired Tomahawk land attack missiles during trials off the coast of the United States.
HMS *Ambush* then saw an extended period of operation service in the North Atlantic and Mediterranean supporting NATO and allied naval forces. In 2016 her conning tower was damaged in a collision with a civilian merchant vessel near Gibraltar.
The submarine has been berthed at Faslane naval base since 2022 undergoing long term maintenance.
(MOD CROWN COPYRIGHT)

ASTUTE-CLASS NUCLEAR POWERED ATTACK SUBMARINE

Displacement Submerged: 7,800 ton

Length: 97m (318ft 3in)

Beam: 11.3m (37ft 1in)

Draught: 10m (32ft 10in)

Propulsion: Single Rolls-Royce PWR 2 nuclear reactor

Speed: 30kts (56kph; 35mph), submerged

Range/Endurance: Unlimited in terms of propulsion, air, and water, based on the amount of food carried and endurance of the crew

Complement: 98 (capacity for 109)

Armament: Stowage for up to 38 weapons, including combination of Tomahawk Block IV cruise missiles and Spearfish heavyweight torpedoes

Despite being the Royal Navy's second newest submarine, HMS *Audacious* has been out of action for more than a year because no dry dock is available at Devonport dockyard to repair her.
The submarine's construction was delayed by the introduction of new features and technology. She was placed in the water at the Devonshire Dock basin in 2017, but it was three more years until the submarine finally sailed from Barrow-in-Furness in April 2020, at the height of COVID-19 pandemic. Further trials and tests took place at Faslane naval base to allow the submarine to be formally commissioned into the fleet in September 2021.
In early 2022, she set sail for an extended deployment to the Mediterranean Sea working with NATO and allied naval forces. This included rest and maintenance periods at Limassol on Cyprus and the US naval base at Souda Bay on Crete.
HMS *Audacious* returned to Britain in the spring of 2023 and was almost immediately moved to Devonport for essential maintenance work. Delays in repairing dry docks at the naval base meant the submarine had to be tied up for an extended period. Some work has been underway but there is no sign of a dry dock becoming available. (TIM RIPLEY)

THE FLEET TODAY

The Carriers

HMS *Queen Elizabeth* and HMS *Prince of Wales*

RIGHT: HMS *Prince of Wales* **led a NATO task group operating off the coast of north Norway during Exercise Steadfast Defender in February and March 2024.**
(MOD CROWN COPYRIGHT)

After a gap of seven years, the Royal Navy returned to the aircraft carrier game in 2017 when HMS *Queen Elizabeth* was floated out of Rosyth dockyard in Scotland.

She was joined two years later by HMS *Prince of Wales* and since then the Royal Navy has been building up their capability to operate fast jet combat aircraft during complex missions. Both carriers are built to a common design and share many features.

The 65,000-ton warships are designed primarily as strike carriers to project air power around the world. They are equipped to routinely embark a mix of 36 Lockheed Martin F-35B Lightning combat jets and AgustaWestland Merlin MH2/HC4 helicopters. In surge situations, around a dozen more airframes could be embarked.

Their fight decks are optimised to operate the vertical take-off and landing (VTOL) variant of the F-35. Both ships have ski jumps fitted so the jets do not have use their lift fans to take off. They do not have arrestor wires fitted so the F-35Bs usually have to use their lift fans to recover onto the deck, but the option is available to make rolling landings to allow the jets to bring back unused ordnance. Hot jet wash from the lift fan could potentially damage the ship's flight

BELOW: RAF F-35B combat jets practiced strike missions against shore targets inside the Norwegian Arctic circle during Exercise Steadfast Defender.
(MOD CROWN COPYRIGHT)

68 ROYAL NAVY YEARBOOK 2024–25

THE FLEET TODAY

decks so they have been coated in heat-resistant materials.

The ships use a distinctive two-island design, with the forward island housing the ship's bridge and the rear island housing the flight control centre. A unique system of information displays on the flight control island allows orders to be issued to flight deck personnel.

Below the flight deck, a large hanger deck is available to store aircraft and conduct maintenance. A system of automated lifts is installed so munitions can be safely and quickly moved from magazines deep in the ship to the flight deck or hanger deck for loading on to aircraft.

Both ships are home ported at Portsmouth naval base, where specialist facilities have been built to accommodate them and the channel into the base is regularly dredged to keep it open for the two big flat tops.

The Royal Navy's flagship, HMS *Queen Elizabeth*, was out of action for the first half of 2024 after she suffered a major propulsion malfunction as she sailed for a major NATO exercise.

She was put into dry dock in Babcock's Rosyth dockyard for repairs but left port in July 2024 and returned to Portsmouth. HMS *Prince of Wales* took part in a major NATO exercise in February and March, before returning to Portsmouth for a period of maintenance. She is to put to sea in the autumn to begin work up training before leading the Carrier Strike Group 2025 deployment to the Far East in 2025.

ABOVE: HMS *Queen Elizabeth* was rapidly stripped of her air group and supplies after breaking down in January 2024 and remained in Portsmouth while HMS *Prince of Wales* took her place on Exercise Steadfast Defender. (DEREK FOX)

BELOW: HMS *Prince of Wales* is refuelled at sea from RFA *Tidesurge* during Exercise Steadfast Defender. (MOD CROWN COPYRIGHT)

QUEEN ELIZABETH-CLASS AIRCRAFT CARRIERS

Displacement:	65,000 tons
Length:	280m (920ft)
Beam:	73m (240ft)
Draught:	11m (36ft)
Propulsion:	Two Rolls-Royce Marine Trent MT30 36 MW (48,000hp) gas turbine generator units and four Wärtsilä diesel generator sets (two x 12,000hp and two x 15,000 hp)
Speed:	46kph (25kts)
Capacity:	1,600, of which 679 are usually the ship's crew
Armament:	Three Phalanx CIWS, four 30mm DS30M Mk2 guns and six mini-guns
Aircraft carried:	40 aircraft and helicopters: (65+ aircraft surge capacity)

www.keymilitary.com 69

THE FLEET TODAY

Defending the Fleet

Type 45 Destroyers

The lead ship of the Type 45-class, HMS *Daring* has spent the past four years undergoing a major overhaul and installation of new power units to deal with electrical systems shortfalls. It was the pathfinder for the Power Improvement Project (PIP), with early phases of the work being undertaken at Cammell Laird shipyard in Birkenhead. She is now in the final phase of this work at Portsmouth, ahead of re-joining the fleet later in 2024. (MOD CROWN COPYRIGHT)

HMS *Defender* is now two years into a three year-long refit, during which she is to undergo the Power Improvement Programme (PIP) electrical upgrade, integration of the Sea Ceptor air defence missile system, and incorporate the new Naval Strike Missile to enhance its anti-ship capability. (DEREK FOX)

In May 2023 HMS *Dauntless* deployed to the Caribbean on a six-month counter-drug operation and to stand ready to assist British Overseas Territories in the region in case of hurricanes.
On her return to Portsmouth in December 2023, HMS *Dauntless* moved into a period of extended maintenance. This is expected to extend into 2024 and could involved the installation of the Naval Strike Missile anti-ship weapon. The ship was the first Type 45 to undergo the Power Improvement Programme (PIP) in 2022. (DEREK FOX)

THE FLEET TODAY

HMS *Dragon* is undergoing a Power Improvement Programme (PIP) upgrade to her electrical system in Portsmouth dockyard. This is expected to be completed late in 2024, when she will begin a period of work up training to return to the fleet.

The ship has a strong affiliation with Wales and famously sports large artwork representing a Welsh dragon on either side of her bow. Before she entered her refit period, HMS *Dragon* played a starring role in the James Bond movie, *No Time to Die*. (MOD CROWN COPYRIGHT)

TYPE 45/DARING-CLASS GUIDED MISSILE DESTROYER

Displacement: 8,500 tonnes

Length: 152.4m (500ft)

Beam: 21.2m (69ft 7in)

Draught: 7.4m (24ft 3in)

Propulsion: Two × Rolls-Royce WR-21 gas turbines, ((28,800 shp), two × Wärtsilä 12V200 diesel generators (2,700 shp)

Speed: In excess of 32kts, (59kph; 37mph)

Range: In excess of 7,000nm (13,000km)

Complement: 191

Sensors:

SAMPSON multi-function air tracking radar (Type 1045)

S1850M 3-D air surveillance radar (Type 1046)

Armament:

Anti-air missiles: PAAMS air-defence system comprising, 48 × Sylver Vertical Launching System A50 for combination of Aster 15 missiles (range 1.7–30km) and Aster 30 missiles (range 3–120km)

Guns: 1 × 4.5in Mark 8 naval gun, 2 × 30mm DS30B guns, 2 × 20mmPhalanx CIWS, 2 × Miniguns,

Aircraft carried: 1 × Wildcat HMA2 or 1 × Merlin HM2

HMS *Diamond* has seen an action-packed year, operating in the Red Sea as part of the international task force protecting merchant shipping from attack by Houthi rebels. She returned to Portsmouth in June 2024 after spending nearly six months committed to the Red Sea operation.

The ship was one of the first Type 45s to suffer electrical power problems, which caused her to return early from an operational deployment to the Middle East in 2017. She is now undergoing a Power Improvement Programme (PIP) refit to improve her electrical system, and this is expected to take at least two years. (DEREK FOX)

In May 2024 HMS *Duncan* sailed from Portsmouth with orders to head to the Red Sea to relieve HMS *Diamond*. Growing tension in the Lebanon led to HMS *Duncan* being diverted to the eastern Mediterranean to join a US-led international task force gathering in case of an evacuation of British nationals from the Middle Eastern country. The ship is the last in line to receive the Power Improvement Programme (PIP) upgrade. (DEREK FOX)

THE FLEET TODAY

Workhorses of the Fleet

Type 23 Frigates

HMS *Portland* has been the Royal Navy's high readiness escort for much of 2024. High points included stepping in at short notice to replace HMS *Somerset* on the major NATO Exercise Steadfast Defender in February 2024 after *Somerset* broke down.

The ship is the second youngest of the remaining Type 23 frigates and is expected to be one of last to be retired in a decade's time. In 2018, she began a three-year-long life extension (LIFEX) refit, which included the installation of the Sea Ceptor surface-to-air missile system, 997 surveillance radar, 1084 navigational radar and the 2150 hull-mounted sonar. (MOD CROWN COPYRIGHT)

HMS *St Albans* is the youngest Type 23 and was only commissioned into the fleet in 2000. Consequently, she is expected to soldier-on in the fleet until 2035 and has been put through a major life extension (LIFEX) refit to ensure she can remain in service for at least another decade.

This refit took just under five years and Babcock only handed her back to the fleet in March 2024 to allow sea trials to begin. 'The Saint' as she is affectionately known by her crew is expected to be declared fully operational during 2025. (MOD CROWN COPYRIGHT)

HMS *Iron Duke* is the second oldest Type 23 remaining in service, and she underwent a long life extension (LIFEX) refit that concluded in 2022. The ship then began work up training to return to duty, which concluded in early 2024 with a period of fleet training by the FOST organisation.

She has been active in British waters during the summer of 2024 and is expected to be deployed on operations in the near future. As the ship is a general-purpose variant and is not equipped with Type 2087 towed array sonar, she must be a strong candidate to replace HMS *Lancaster* in the Middle East when that ship's three-year long deployment comes to an end in 2025, as anti-submarine warfare capabilities are not a priority in this region. (DEREK FOX)

THE FLEET TODAY

HMS *Lancaster* is the oldest Type 23 frigate still in Royal Navy service and is one of two of the class remaining that have not been fitted with the 2087 towed array sonar to enhance their anti-submarine capability.

In 2022 she sailed to the Arabian Gulf to begin a three-year long extended deployment at Britain's naval base on the island state of Bahrain. Under the Royal Navy's forward deployment concept, her crew is rotated every four to five months. This replaced the previous concept of sailing warships back and forth to the Middle East every six months.

Over the past year the frigate has been heavily involved in regional security operations in responses to the conflict in Gaza. The ship has patrolled the Arabian Gulf and Indian Ocean to secure international trade.

Once she completes her deployment in 2025, it is expected that the ship will be retired rather than be put through an expensive refit. (MOD CROWN COPYRIGHT)

HMS *Kent* deployed to the Pacific region in 2021 alongside HMS *Queen Elizabeth* as part of the Carrier Strike Group 2021 deployment. On her return, the frigate operated as an escort for carriers in European waters.

In April 2024, HMS *Kent* began a refit and upkeep period in the Devonport dockyard frigate support centre. This will include a power generation and machinery upgrade as well as remedial work to her hull. (DEREK FOX)

HMS *Northumberland* entered the Devonport dockyard frigate support centre in March 2024 for maintenance upkeep after a period of intense operations over the previous four years. As one of the seven remaining Type 2087 towed array sonar frigates, HMS *Northumberland* was much in demand for anti-submarine operations in the North Atlantic region.

Reports are emerging that inspections of the frigate have determined that she is uneconomic to repair, so rather than spending more than £100m to complete her upkeep period, the ship could be scrapped in the very near future. (MOD CROWN COPYRIGHT)

TYPE 23/DUKE-CLASS FRIGATE
Type: Anti-submarine warfare frigate
Displacement: 4,900 tonnes (4,800 long tons)
Length: 133m (436ft 4in)
Beam: 16.1m (52ft 10in)
Draught: 7.3m (23ft 11in)
Propulsion: Two × Rolls-Royce Marine Spey SM1C
Speed: In excess of 28kts (52kph; 32mph)
Range: 7,500nm (14,000km; 9,000 miles)
Complement: 185
Armament:
Anti-air missiles: Single 32-cell Sea Ceptor GWS 35 Vertical Launching System (VLS) canisters for 32 missiles (1–25+ km)
Anti-submarine torpedoes: Two × twin 12.75in (324mm) Sting Ray torpedo tubes
Guns: 1 × BAE 4.5in Mk 8 naval gun, 2 × 30mm DS30M Mk2 guns, or 2 × 30mm DS30B guns, 2 × Miniguns,
Aircraft carried: 1 × Wildcat HMA2 or 1 × Merlin HM2

THE FLEET TODAY

After completing a four-year-long life extension (LIFEX) refit in 2022, HMS *Somerset* has been dogged by technical problems and mechanical breakdowns.

A rudder bearing failed which required a three month long dry dock period in Rosyth for repairs late in 2022. The ship was scheduled to be fitted with the new anti-ship Naval Strike Missile (NSM), but this was thrown into doubt after she suffered another major breakdown in February 2024 while en route to join NATO's Exercise Steadfast Defender.

Since then, she has been undergoing repairs at Devonport dockyard but was sighted at sea in July and August while undergoing trials, ahead of finally rejoining the fleet. (DEREK FOX)

In 2021, HMS *Sutherland* entered the Devonport dockyard frigate support centre to begin a life extension (LIFEX) programme to incorporate the new Sea Ceptor missile and have a new power system upgrade. Repairs to her hull involved 11,500 welds and the insertion of 700 pieces of new steel.

The ship was floated out of the support centre's dry dock in March 2024 and Babcock engineers are in the process of handing her back to the Royal Navy so she can begin work up training to rejoin the fleet later this year. (MOD CROWN COPYRIGHT)

HMS *Richmond* was the Royal Navy's high readiness frigate in early 2024. She was scrambled to head to the Red Sea in January 2024 to temporarily take over from HMS *Diamond* in the international task force protecting merchant shipping from Houthi attacks. Once HMS *Richmond* was on station, the Type 45 destroyer could transit to Gibraltar to re-load her Sea Viper missiles. The Type 23 frigate remained on station until April 2024 and engaged Houthi forces on several occasions. In March 2024, the ship used the Sea Ceptor missile in combat for the first time to engage two Houthi attack drones.

The ship returned to Devonport to start a period of maintenance but was deployed again in August when she was activated to escort Chinese warships through the English Channel. (MOD CROWN COPYRIGHT)

THE FLEET TODAY

Specialist Ships
Assault Ships, Mine Countermeasures and Patrol Vessels

Albion-Class Assault Ships

THE TWO Albion-class assault ships, HMS *Albion,* and HMS *Bulwark* were ordered in 1996 to replace the aging 1960s vintage ships HMS *Fearless* and HMS *Intrepid*.

The assault ships play a key role in Royal Marines amphibious operations, allowing heavy vehicles and landing craft to be carried long distances inside their large well deck or internal dock. They also have command and control facilities to allow senior amphibious commanders and their staff to be embarked to direct major operations.

Since the two ships entered service in 2003 and 2004, they have played a prominent role in many Royal Navy and Royal Marine operations. In 2015, HMS *Bulwark* was dispatched to the central Mediterranean to take part in a major operation to rescue migrants crossing from Libya. After the Royal Navy retired its last Invincible-class aircraft carrier, HMS *Illustrious*, in 2014, the two assault ships took turns to be the fleet flagship, with the flat top amphibious assault ship HMS *Ocean*. Once HMS *Ocean* retired in 2018, HMS *Albion* assumed the role of flag ship for three years until HMS *Queen Elizabeth* was fully operational.

LEFT: HMS *Albion* **operated as a floating base for Royal Marine raiding crafts on several major NATO exercises off the coast of Norway and in the Baltic Sea.**
(MOD CROWN COPYRIGHT)

As a result of a round of defence budget cuts in 2010, the Royal Navy was only able to keep one of the ships in service at any point in time. The non-operational ship was placed in what was termed 'extended readiness' for three years at a time in Devonport dockyard. A skeleton crew was maintained onboard, who in theory could bring the ship back into action in an emergency.

A handover of duty was scheduled for 2023-24 when HMS *Albion* completed a series of NATO exercises. However, personnel shortages across the Royal Navy meant HMS *Bulwark* was not reactivated. In early 2024, government ministers claimed at least one of the ships would return to duty later in the decade.

LEFT: HMS *Bulwark* **played a central role in the 2015 migrant rescue operation in the Mediterranean, when she plucked more than 2,800 from the sea.**
(MOD CROWN COPYRIGHT)

www.keymilitary.com 75

THE FLEET TODAY

Mine Countermeasures Vessels

HMS *Hurworth* is one of the six remaining Hunt-class mine countermeasures vessels remaining in Royal Navy service. She is currently home-based at Portsmouth and has been operating in European waters supporting NATO allies or monitoring the underwater environment close to Britain's naval bases. (DEREK FOX)

HMS *Brocklesby* is currently undergoing a major refit at Portsmouth dockyard to enhance her ability to embark autonomous and remote/offboard mine hunting systems. She returned from an extended tour of duty in the Arabian Gulf in 2021. (DEREK FOX)

HMS *Cattistock* is currently home ported at Portsmouth naval base and has been operating in European waters supporting NATO allies or monitoring the underwater environment close to Britain's naval bases. She underwent a major refit from 2021 to 2023. In November 2023, HMS *Cattistock* was involved in a major operation in the North Sea with vessels and aircraft from NATO allies to monitor vulnerable undersea critical infrastructure. (DEREK FOX)

THE FLEET TODAY

HMS *Ledbury* is the oldest active commissioned ship in the Royal Navy, being launched in December 1979 and commissioned into the fleet in June 1981.

The ship is currently undergoing a refit and upgrade at Portsmouth naval base that will allow her to remain in service to the end of the decade when the Hunt-class are due to be replaced by unscrewed mine hunting systems.

Her refit is scheduled to be complete later in 2024, when she will return to the fleet and then deploy to the Arabian Gulf to join Operation Kipion.

The refit is being carried out by BAE Systems, supported by WEMEC. This involves the installation of new engines, hydraulic systems and control and monitoring systems tailored to deal with the unique electromagnetic challenges posed by their role. (MOD CROWN COPYRIGHT)

HMS *Middleton* is currently forward deployed in the Middle East at the Royal Navy's base on the Gulf Island state f Bahrain.

The mine hunter operates as part of the Royal Navy task force in the region, which is dubbed Operation Kipion. Briefly, during the spring of 2024, HMS *Middleton* was the only operational mine countermeasures vessel in the Gulf after her sister ships, HMS *Bangor*, and HMS *Chiddingfold*, were involved in a high-profile collision.

Before her deployment on Operation Kipion in 2021, the ship underwent a major upgrade. (GLENN SALT)

HMS *Bangor* is the last surviving Sandown-class mine countermeasures (CMC) ship. The ship is currently forward deployed in Bahrain as part of Operation Kipion and was damaged in a collision with HMS *Chiddingfold* in January 2024 but has since been repaired.

She was commissioned into the fleet in 1999 and is due to be retired next year as part of the Royal Navy's drive to replace crewed MCM ships with robot capabilities to reduce costs and risks to human crew members.

They will be replaced with autonomous mine hunting systems and specialised 'motherships' deployed either by the Royal Fleet Auxiliary vessels or new-build ships. (BRUCE DAVIDSON)

HMS *Chiddingfold* sailed to the Arabian Gulf in mid-2020 to begin an extended period of duty with the British mine countermeasures flotilla operating in the Middle East. From the British naval base on Bahrain, HMS *Jufair*, the flotilla protects freedom of navigation for merchant shipping across the region.

The ship was involved in an accident in Bahrain's Mina al Salman harbour in January 2024 which was caught on video and went viral on social media. HMS *Chiddingfold* appeared to run out of control and reversed into HMS *Bangor*, causing damage to her glass fibre hull. (MOD CROWN COPYRIGHT)

THE FLEET TODAY

Survey and Research Vessels

HMS *Protector* is the Royal Navy's dedicated ice patrol ship and has an important role to play in protecting Britain's Antarctic territories. She is the modern-day successor to HMS *Endurance* of 1982 Falklands war fame.

She was originally built by a Norwegian company for polar research and has a strengthened hull to protect her when sailing through ice floes. After being temporarily leased in 2011 to fill the gap left by the retirement of the second HMS *Endurance*, the ship was purchased outright in 2013 for £51m.

The ship routinely deploys for extended patrols in the South Atlantic to demonstrate British claims to be the sovereignty of its territories in the region and to assist polar experts from the British Antarctic Survey in scientific research.
(MOD CROWN COPYRIGHT)

HMS *Scott* is the Royal Navy's only operational underwater survey vessel. It is purpose designed and equipped to carry out detailed surveys of the ocean floor to aid Royal Navy and allied underwater operations. Its specialist equipment includes an advanced high-resolution, multi-beam sonar system to create underwater maps.

The ship was commissioned in 1997 and was expected to retire in 2023 but was given an extension for a decade because of delays in bringing new Multi-Role Ocean Surveillance ships into service. An additional role is to supplement the ice patrol ship, HMS *Protector*, when she has to return from the Antarctic for maintenance.
(MOD CROWN COPYRIGHT)

XV Patrick Blackett is an experimental ship used by the Royal Navy's NavyX division as a test bed for new technologies, including unmanned underwater vehicles, unmanned surface vehicles, and quantum navigation. She is named after Patrick Blackett, a Royal Navy veteran and Nobel Prize-winning British physicist. (DEREK FOX)

THE FLEET TODAY

River-class Offshore Patrol Vessels

The first of the River-class offshore patrol vessel, HMS *Tyne*, was commissioned into the Royal Navy in July 2003. The three Batch 1 vessels, HMS *Tyne*, HMS *Severn*, and HMS *Mersey*, initially served in fishery protection duties in British home waters until 2017 when the Ministry of Defence announced the ships would be retired to free up their crews to serve on other warships. This decision was reversed in 2018, and the ships were brought back into frontline service to help protect Britain's exclusive economic maritime zone in the aftermath of the country's departure from the European Union. (MOD CROWN COPYRIGHT)

As well as helping to protect Britain's maritime interests in home waters, HMS *Severn* also has a secondary role as a navigation training ship. In May 2021, she played a prominent role in a confrontation in Jersey harbour between Channel Islands and French fishermen. (DEREK FOX)

HMS *Mersey* is currently undergoing a major overhaul in Portsmouth naval base to extend her in service beyond 2028. The ship and her two sister Batch 1 offshore patrol vessels are home ported in Portsmouth to provide a naval presence in British home waters and to support maritime law enforcement and environmental agencies. (MOD CROWN COPYRIGHT)

RIVERCLASS PATROL BOAT
Displacement:
Batch 1: 1,700 tons
Batch 2: 2,000 tons
Length:
Batch 1: 79.5m (260ft 10in)
Batch 2: 90.5m (296ft 11in)
Beam:
Batch 1: 13.5m (44ft 3in)
Batch 2: 13.5m (44ft 3in)
Draught:
Batch 1: 3.8m (12ft 6in)
Batch 2: 3.8m (12ft 6in)
Speed:
Batch 1: 20kts (37kph; 23mph)
Batch 2: 25kts (46kph; 29mph)
Range:
Batch 2: 5,500nm (10,200km; 6,300 miles)
Armament:
Batch 1: One Oerlikon 20mm cannon, two × General Purpose Machine Guns
Batch 2: One Bushmaster 30mm cannon, two × Miniguns, two × General Purpose Machine Guns
Aviation facilities:
Batch 2: Merlin-capable flight deck

THE FLEET TODAY

After returning from duty in the Falklands in the autumn of 2023, HMS *Medway* has been undergoing a period of intense maintenance at the Royal Navy base in Gibraltar. The Batch 2 River-class offshore patrol vessels use 'The Rock' as a maintenance and support base for operations in the Mediterranean, Caribbean and South Atlantic. (MOD CROWN COPYRIGHT)

HMS *Trent* was diverted to the Cayman Islands in July 2024 to help provide humanitarian assistance after the Caribbean region was hit by Hurricane Beryl. The vessel is normally based in Gibraltar but had been detached to serve as the Royal Navy's Caribbean Guard Ship. (MOD CROWN COPYRIGHT)

HMS *Spey* departed Portsmouth in September 2021, along with HMS *Tamar*, on a five-year mission to show the White Ensign in the Indo-Pacific region. Into 2024, the ship has been operating in the Indian Ocean and East China Sea. This included a dry dock period in Japan in May 2024. (MOD CROWN COPYRIGHT)

Along with HMS *Spey*, HMS *Tamar* departed Portsmouth in September 2021, to operate in the Indo-Pacific region for five years. During 2024, she has made visits to Australia and South Sea islands, including the Pitcairn Islands. (HAMMERSFAN)

Since 2020, HMS *Forth* has been the Falklands Islands guard ship, providing a permanent naval presence to protect Britain's South Atlantic Territories. For six months in 2023, she underwent maintenance in Gibraltar and was temporarily replaced by HMS *Medway*. (MOD CROWN COPYRIGHT)

ROYAL FLEET AUXILIARY

Supporting the Fleet

Tankers, Landing Ships and Underwater Operations

The Royal Fleet Auxiliary provides the Royal Navy's modern day 'fleet train' to supply its warships with fuel, munitions, water, and other supplies without them having to return to port. Here the fleet tanker, RFA *Tiderace*, conducts a dual replenishment at sea (RAS), with HMS *Lancaster* and HMS *Westminster*, passing fuel and water over pipelines, during a major NATO exercise off the northern coast of Norway in March 2021. (MOD CROWN COPYRIGHT)

Food and ammunition to replenish Royal Navy carrier battlegroups is carried by the RFA *Fort Victoria*, which is fitted with RAS equipment to allow supplies to be passed to warships underway. She is the last dedicated solid support ship in the Royal Fleet Auxiliary and is essential to allow the Royal Navy's two aircraft carriers to be able to operate far from home, without having to put into port. The ship is starting to show her 30-year age and is currently undergoing a major refit and maintenance period at the Cammell Laird shipyard on the Mersey. Reports are emerging suggesting she might not be in a fit condition to support the Carrier Strike Group 2025 deployment to the Pacific region next year. Three new solid support ships have been ordered to replace her from 2030. (MOD CROWN COPYRIGHT)

ROYAL FLEET AUXILLIARY SHIPS 2024

Tide-Class Fleet Tankers
RFA *Tidespring*
RFA *Tiderace*
RFA *Tidesurge*
RFA *Tideforce*

Bay-Class Landing Ships
RFA *Cardigan Bay*
RFA *Lyme Bay*
RFA *Mounts Bay*

Aviation Support/Littoral Strike Ship
RFA *Argus*

Solid Support Ship
RFA *Fort Victoria*

Specialist Vessels
RFA *Stirling Castle*
RFA *Proteus*
RFA *Wave Knight*

Royal Navy helicopter pilots and deck crews receive training in carrier aviation operations on board RFA *Argus*. The ship was originally built as the container ship, MV *Contender Bezant* in 1980 and two years later was requisitioned for the Falklands conflict. In 1984, she was converted into an aviation training ship and in the 1991 Gulf War was used as floating hospital. In 2022 the ship was given a new role as the littoral strike role ship, to act as a floating base for Royal Marine Commandos and their supporting battlefield helicopters. This included fitting a single Phalanx 20mm close-in-weapon-system as part of her self-defence armament. During the spring and summer of 2024, the ship carried a Royal Marines Littoral Response Group to Australia for a major exercise. (MOD CROWN COPYRIGHT)

ROYAL FLEET AUXILIARY

Bay-Class Dock Landing Ship

The Royal Fleet Auxiliary operates a fleet of three Bay-class dock landing ships to support Royal Marine amphibious forces and Royal Navy mine countermeasures. In the summer of 2024, RFA *Mounts Bay* deployed to the Mediterranean to take over from RAF *Cardigan Bay*, which was operating with an international task force deployed in the region. The Bay-class ships have a large rear flight deck to allow several helicopters to load troops and cargo. (MOD CROWN COPYRIGHT)

In May 2024, RFA *Cardigan Bay* relocated from the Arabian Gulf, where she had been supporting the Royal Navy mine countermeasures flotilla based in Bahrain. The ship spent three months operating off Gaza providing logistic support for the US military's harbour, delivering humanitarian aid to the war-torn territory. This mission concluded in July 2024 and RFA *Cardigan Bay* then joined the international task force in the eastern Mediterranean in case an evacuation of civilians was needed from Lebanon. The ship's landing craft were used to move personnel and cargo to and from the US military harbour anchored off Gaza. (MOD CROWN COPYRIGHT)

ROYAL FLEET AUXILIARY

In the autumn of 2023, Littoral Response Group (South) sailed for a year-long deployment that would eventually see RFA *Lyme Bay* and RAF *Argus* participating in a major amphibious exercise in northern Australia. En route, LSG(S) spent several months in the eastern Mediterranean after the outbreak of the Gaza war in October 2023 in case an evacuation was needed of civilians from the region. In March 2024, the LRG(S) moved down the Red Sea through the battle zone between allied naval forces and Houthi rebel forces, before heading to India for exercises with the Indian naval forces. Royal Marines of 40 Commando were embarked in the two ships throughout the deployment. (MOD CROWN COPYRIGHT)

British Bay-class ships are based on the Royal Schelde Enforcer, a joint project between The Netherlands and Spain that resulted in the Rotterdam-class and Galicia-class amphibious warfare ships. The main difference is that the British ships have no helicopter hangar.

The rear well deck, or dock, of the Bay-class ships can allow access to landing craft. This dock can accommodate up to two landing craft and two Mexeflote pontons can be suspended from the ship's side. Two 30-ton cranes are fitted between the superstructure and the flight deck. Internal passages are wide enough to allow two fully kitted marines to pass each other. (MOD CROWN COPYRIGHT)

www.keymilitary.com **83**

ROYAL FLEET AUXILIARY

Tide-Class Fleet Tankers

The Royal Fleet Auxiliary's four Tide-class fleet tankers entered service from 2017 under the Military Afloat Reach and Sustainability (MARS) project. RFA *Tidespring*, the first of its class, and the other three ships were built in Daewoo's yard in South Korea and fitted with UK-specific equipment at A&P's Falmouth yard.

The ships were fitted with dual replenishment at sea (RAS) equipment so they could pass fuel and water to warships sailing along both sides. (MOD CROWN COPYRIGHT)

RFA *Tideforce* was the last ship of the Tide-class, and she entered Royal Fleet Auxiliary service in July 2019. Since then, she has supported Royal Navy deployments in European, North American, and Caribbean waters, including operating with the aircraft carrier HMS *Queen Elizabeth*. The Tide-class replaced the old Wave-class tankers, of which only one remains, RFA *Wave Knight*. She is laid up in Portsmouth, pending disposal. (TIM RIPLEY)

In February and March 2024, RFA *Tidesurge* supported the aircraft carrier HMS *Prince of Wales* as she sailed into the Arctic Circle during NATO's Exercise Steadfast Defender. The tanker also passed fuel to other Royal Navy and allied warships during the six-week-long exercise which tested NATO plans to reinforce Norway in time of conflict with Russia. (MOD CROWN COPYRIGHT)

Specialist Ships

RFA *Proteus* is a former oil industry supply vessel, the MV *Topaz Tangaroa*, and was bought for the Royal Fleet Auxiliary in 2023 for conversion into a Multi-Role Ocean Surveillance Ship (MROSS).
After undergoing a dry dock period in the Cammell Laird shipyard on the Mersey to modify her for the MROSS role, she formally entered Royal Fleet Auxiliary service in October 2023. The ship is intended to deploy multiple remotely operated vehicles (ROVs) to monitor underwater infrastructure under threat from hostile attack. It had originally been intended to build two new MROSS for this important new role, but it was found to be cheaper and quicker to convert civilian vessels. (DEREK FOX)

RFA *Stirling Castle* was acquired by the Ministry of Defence in 2023 for £40m to act as a 'mother ship' for autonomous mine hunting systems. The ship was formerly the MV *Island Crown* and was used as an offshore supply vessel in the oil and gas industry. After being bought by the MoD, the ship was modified for its new role in Devonport naval base. She was formally commissioned into the Royal Fleet Auxiliary in April 2024.
In July 2023, the ship conducted its first trials with three of the Royal Navy's autonomous vessels, *Apollo*, *Hydra* and *Hazard*. However, from January to March 2024, RFA *Stirling Castle* undertook operational sea training in preparation for work with the Mine and Threat Exploitation Group at the Faslane naval base. It is intended that the ship will be ready to fill the gap that will be created following the retirement of the Royal Navy's Sandown-class mine hunters in 2025. (MOD CROWN COPYRIGHT)

FLEET AIR ARM

Fly Navy

Jets, Sub Hunters, Junglies, and Drones

ABOVE: F-35B Lightning II jump jets form the core of the air groups embarked on the Royal Navy's Queen Elizabeth-class aircraft carriers. (MOD CROWN COPYRIGHT)

BELOW: The Royal Navy's Merlin HM2 maritime helicopter is designed to find, identify and kill enemy submarines. Development began in the 1980s and the type started to enter service a decade later. To find submarines it has a dipping sonar and can drop fields of sonobuoys. Its primary weapon is the Stingray homing torpedo. The original version, the HM1, was upgraded to the HM2 a decade ago. (MOD CROWN COPYRIGHT)

Royal Navy aviators have been flying off ships for more than a century and are now leading the development of unmanned aerial vehicles, or drones, to take the Fleet Air Arm (FAA) into the 21st century.

The FAA is the Royal Navy's aviation branch, and it operates the full spectrum of naval aviation – fast jets, maritime helicopters, air assault helicopters and drones. At their shore bases, FAA aircraft and helicopters are grouped into Naval Air Squadrons (NAS), but they are routinely deployed in small detachments, or ship's flights, for operation missions on warships and Royal Fleet Auxiliary support ships.

FAA helicopters are now concentrated at two main operating bases and the Lockheed Martin F-35B Lightning II jump jets share a base with the Royal Air Force.

Royal Naval Air Station (RNAS) Culdrose in Cornwall is home to the FAA's AgustaWestland Merlin HM2 anti-submarine warfare (ASW) helicopters and RNAS Yeovilton is home to the Commando Helicopter Force, as well as the two squadrons that operate the Leonardo Wildcat HMA2 maritime helicopters.

Potential naval aviators are trained in the tri-service Military Flying Training Service pipeline that is run by the Royal Air Force's 22 Group. Successful students then move to type conversion run by the Royal Navy at Culdrose and Yeovilton.

The core effort of the FAA is to generate aircraft, helicopters, and crews for the air groups on the two Queen Elizabeth-class aircraft carriers. After a decade-long 'carrier holiday', the Royal Navy is well and truly back in the 'carrier game'. Its attention is now turning to embracing new unmanned technology to fly off the decks of Royal Navy warships.

FLEET AIR ARM INVENTORY, OCTOBER 2024			
	Total	**Forward Fleet**	**Sustainment Fleet**
Rotary-wing Platforms			
Dauphin	**2**	2	
Merlin HM2	**29**	18	11
Merlin HC4/4A	**25**	21	4
Wildcat HMA2	**28**	21	7
Fixed-wing Platforms			
Avenger T1	**4**	4	
Tutor T1	**5**	5	

Notes
Forward Fleet: Airframes in day-to-day use
Sustainment Fleet: Airframes undergoing depth maintenance or in storage
Source: UK Armed Forces Equipment and Formations annual report by UK Ministry of Defence, FOI Documents

FLEET AIR ARM

Sub Hunting Merlins

The Merlin HM2 is the main helicopter embarked on the Queen Elizabeth-class aircraft carriers, up to eight of the machines are usually deployed onboard whenever the ships operate as part of a fully formed carrier battlegroup. (MOD CROWN COPYRIGHT)

MERLIN HM2 MARITIME HELICOPTER

Powerplant: Three × Rolls-Royce Turbomeca RTM322-01 turboshafts

Length: 19.53m (64ft 1in)

Height: 6.62m (21ft 9in)

Max take-off weight: 14,600kg (32,187lb)

Cruise speed: 278kph (173mph, 150kts)

Range: 833km (518 miles, 450nm)

Endurance: Five hours

Crew: Two pilots, one observer

Avionics:

Selex Galileo Blue Kestrel 5000 maritime surveillance radar

ASW Sensors

Active/passive sonobuoys

Thales 2189 dipping sonar array

MX-15 FLIR turret

Armament:

Bombs: Four x Stingray homing torpedoes or Mk 11 depth charges

Door guns: One x .50cal machine gun

The arrival of the Merlin HM1 saw the 814 Naval Air Squadron reformed in 2001 to operate the new advanced maritime helicopter. It was subsequently re-equipped with the upgraded Merlin HM2 in 2014. Personnel from the disbanded 829 Naval Air Squadron were incorporated into the unit in 2018, and 814 Squadron took over its role to supply independent flights on frigates and destroyers, as well as operating in the ASW role from Prestwick on the Clyde estuary. It is nicknamed the 'Flying Tigers' and a Tiger insignia is painted on the nose of its helicopters. (MOD CROWN COPYRIGHT)

FLEET AIR ARM

820 Naval Air Squadron is now the core maritime helicopter squadron of HMS *Queen Elizabeth*'s air group, hence her nickname, 'The Queen's Squadron'. The squadron embarked on the carrier for her maiden operational Carrier Strike Group deployment to the Far East in 2021. It will transfer to HMS *Prince of Wales* when she takes over the role of fleet flagship in late 2024 ahead of the Carrier Strike Group 2025 deployment to the Far East.
(MOD CROWN COPYRIGHT)

824 Naval Air Squadron was reformed in 2000, and is now the main Merlin training unit, preparing pilots, observers, aircrew, and groundcrew to operate the helicopter in a dedicated training facility at RNAS Culdrose that is equipped with purpose-built simulators. Crews are trained to operate both versions, the anti-submarine HM2 variant and the Crowsnest airborne early warning variant, which is seen here. Its radar is protected inside the inflatable canvas radome, known as the 'bag' during missions.
(MOD CROWN COPYRIGHT)

FLEET AIR ARM

Maritime Wildcats

HMS *Heron* at Yeovilton is home to the Fleet Air Arm's two squadrons that operate the Wildcat HMA2 maritime helicopter. The Royal Navy Wildcat Force is based around two flying squadrons. 815 Naval Air Squadron (NAS) provides flights of one or two of the 28 Wildcat HMA2 maritime variants to be embarked on Royal Navy frigates and destroyers. Wildcat crews are trained to fly the helicopters by instructors from 825 NAS. As well as operating from warships, 815 NAS routinely practices operating from shore bases in Scandinavia and Britain in the anti-ship role, while working with fast attack craft to dominate key maritime choke points. (MOD CROWN COPYRIGHT)

Wildcat HMA2 maritime helicopters are routinely embarked on Type 45 destroyers and Type 23 frigates in the surface surveillance, attack, and utility role. The helicopter packs a powerful punch with up to 16 Martlet laser beam-riding, Lightweight Multirole *Missiles* (LMM) and is soon to be able to fire the Sea Venom heavy guided missile. Its Sea Spray radar allows the helicopter's crew to look for targets out to more than 100km. The helicopter has a clamp under its fuselage that allows it to be secured on a moving ship's landing pad. Once the Wildcat's rotor blades are folded away, the helicopter can be stowed in a Type 23 or 45's hanger. (MOD CROWN COPYRIGHT)

WILDCAT HMA2 MARITIME HELICOPTER

Powerplant: Two × LHTEC CTS800-4N turboshaft 32,187lb

Length: 15.24m (50ft)

Height: 3.73m (12ft 3in)

Maximum speed: 311kph (193mph, 168 kts)

Range: 734 nm

Endurance: 2hr 15min

Crew: Two pilots

Capacity: Six passengers, including door gunner

Avionics: Salex Seaspray maritime surveillance radar

Wescam MX-15Di EO sensor

Armament:

Pintle-mounted machine gun, 7.62mm GPMG or Browning M3M

Air-to-surface missile systems

Up to 20 × Thales Martlet (Lightweight Multirole Missile),

Up to four × MBDA Sea Venom

Guided Weapon (Heavy)

FLEET AIR ARM

Commando Helicopter Force

Dedicated support to the Royal Marines of 3 Commando Brigade is provided by a specialist unit, the Commando Helicopter Force (CHF), based at RNAS Yeovilton. It is provided with its own mobile command centre, logistic support, and cargo handling facilities to allow it to operate from Royal Navy amphibious warships or ashore in combat zones. The CHF reports to the tri-service Joint Aviation Command, which controls all the UK's battlefield helicopters. (MOD CROWN COPYRIGHT)

MERLIN HC4 ASSAULT HELICOPTER

Powerplant: Three × Rolls-Royce Turbomeca RTM322-01 turboshafts

Length: 19.53m (64ft 1in)

Height: 6.62m (21ft 9in)

Max take-off weight: 14,600kg (32,187lb)

Cruise speed: 309kph (192mph)

Range: 1,360km (738nm)

Endurance: Seven hours

Crew: Two pilots, two loadmasters

Capacity: 38 lightly equipped troops or 16 stretcher causalities

Avionics: FLIR Systems Star SAFIRE III EO turret

Armament: Three × pintle-mounted machine gun, 7.62mm GPMG

The CHF's Merlin HC4 troop carrying helicopters operated by 845 and 846 NAS, are variants of the AgustaWestland Merlin, which were transferred from the RAF, starting in 2014. The 25 ex-RAF Merlin HC3/3As have been converted to the HC4/4A configuration under the Merlin Life Sustainment Programme. (MOD CROWN COPYRIGHT)

FLEET AIR ARM

The third unit of the CHF is 847 Naval Air Squadron (NAS), which operates the land variant of the Wildcat, the AH1. It is closely affiliated with 1 Regiment Army Air Corps, which is also based at Yeovilton and operates the Wildcat AH1, sharing training and maintenance facilities. The navy and army Wildcat units share a common pool of 34 AH1 air frames. CHF Wildcats provide Royal Marine commanders with airborne surveillance capabilities, using their nose-mounted thermal imaging sensors to spot enemy troops and vehicles at night or in bad weather. CHF helicopters are also used to move Royal Marines and cargo around the battlefield. (MOD CROWN COPYRIGHT)

WILDCAT AH1 BATTLEFIELD HELICOPTER

Powerplant: Two × LHTEC CTS800-4N turboshaft

Length: 15.24m (50ft)

Height: 3.73m (12ft 3in)

Max take-off weight: 6,000kg (13,228lb)

Maximum speed: 311kph (193mph, 168kts)

Range: 777km (483 miles, 420nm)

Endurance: 2 hr 15 min (4 hr 30 min with auxiliary fuel tanks)

Crew: Two pilots

Capacity: Six passengers, including door gunner

Avionics: Salex Seaspray maritime surveillance radar, Wescam MX-15Di EO sensor

Armament: Pintle-mounted machine gun, e.g. GPMG or Browning M3M

Fleet Air Arm rear cabin crew have a key role to play in CHF Wildcat operations, loading passengers, stowing cargo, and firing 0.50 calibre door mounted machine guns. Royal Marines are routinely posted to 847 NAS as pilots, rear cabin crews and ground personnel. On major operations or exercises, CHF helicopters and personnel have to live and operate in the field from remote airstrips and landing zones. For three months every year, the CHF deploys its Merlin HC4 and Wildcat AH1 to Bardufoss in northern Norway to train to operate in Arctic conditions. (MOD CROWN COPYRIGHT)

FLEET AIR ARM

Carrier Strike

RIGHT: 809 Naval Air Squadron was reformed in December 2023 as the Royal Navy's contribution to the Lightning Force and the F-35 shown here is sporting the squadron's distinctive badge.
(MOD/CROWN COPYRIGHT)

THE ROYAL Navy's growing fleet of Lockheed Martin F-35B Lightning II 5th generation jump jets are based at RAF Marham in Norfolk.

The jets and personnel, drawn from the Royal Air Force and Royal Navy, are all part of the Lightning Force, or LF. It is currently focused on generating aircraft, aircrew, and ground support personnel to provide the air groups for the two Queen Elizabeth-class aircraft carriers.

All parts of the LF are jointly manned by personnel from the two services, rather than operating as distinct RAF or RN units. Currently there is one fully operational F-35B unit, the famous 617 'Dambusters' Squadron, and an operational conversion unit, 207 Squadron. These are both RAF badged units.

In December 2023, a second operational unit, 809 Naval Air Squadron (NAS), was established and is currently being formed. It is scheduled to be declared fully operational by the end of 2025. The training and operations of the LF are closely synchronised with the sailing programme of the aircraft carriers and it is now routine for 617 Squadron to deploy for at least one extended cruise on one of the carriers each year.

RIGHT: The Phoenix Squadron is reborn, and its distinctive badge now adorns its F-35Bs at RAF Marham. Its pilots are also nicknamed 'The Immortals'.
(MOD CROWN COPYRIGHT)

FLEET AIR ARM

Navy Drones

RNAS Culdrose is home to the Royal Navy's only unit equipped with unmanned aerial vehicles (UAV) - 700X Naval Air Squadron (NAS). The squadron has taken the lead in experimenting with UAVs.
In November 2019, the squadron tested two new mini-UAVs - the AeroVironment RQ-20 Puma and the AeroVironment Wasp III - for their suitability to operate in the maritime environment. (MOD CROWN COPYRIGHT)

700X Naval Air Squadron has developed Predannack airfield, close to RNAS Culdrose, as a training facility for testing and innovating with the latest unmanned systems. It currently has a mix of Royal Navy personnel, supported by Royal Marines, civil servants, and contractors. Drone experiments include the flying mini-hobby drones that are bought on the open market and are considered expendable in battle. (MOD CROWN COPYRIGHT)

750 Naval Air Squadron is tasked with providing basic flying training for the Fleet Air Arm's observers using the Avenger T, a version of the Beechcraft King Air 350s, based at RNAS Culdrose. Trainee aircrew observers join for a seven-month period of training in all aspects of airborne navigation, airmanship, and other tactical skills to allow them become mission specialists in Royal Navy maritime helicopters. The training is conducted in classrooms as well as in the air and in a computer-controlled simulator. Upon completion of this course, they will be ready for advanced flying training and will be streamed for their eventual specialisation on the Wildcat HMA2 or Merlin HM2. (MOD CROWN COPYRIGHT)

In March 2023, 700X NAS took delivery of new jet-powered Banshee UAVs capable of flying at up to 400mph. This is a variant of the Banshee Jet 80+ UAV, developed by defence company QinetiQ to simulate threats to aircraft to help the Royal Navy stay at the cutting-edge of air defence operations. (MOD CROWN COPYRIGHT)

ROYAL MARINES

RIGHT: The Royal Marines have a distinguished history stretching back to 1664 and their modern ceremonial uniforms reflect the force's language and battle honours.
(MOD CROWN COPYRIGHT)

BELOW: Operating on and from the sea is the core business of the Royal Marines and this distinguishes them from the ground combat units of the British Army and RAF Regiment.
(MOD CROWN COPYRIGHT)

Britain's elite amphibious force is in the process of a major re-structuring to better equip it to succeed in 21st century conflicts and crisis.

The new organisation is dubbed the Future Commando Force, and it is has seen almost every aspect of the Royal Marines transformed. Under its old concept, 3 Commando Brigade was the Royal Marines core fighting formation. It was configured and equipped to carry out brigade-sized amphibious operations against enemy coastlines.

The Future Commando Force calls for the Royal Marines to operate in smaller units, in a mix of environments and operational scenarios. At the heart of the concept is the idea that the Royal Navy and Royal Marines have to be able to dominate littoral regions around the world, including operating in small boats, in helicopters, or launching raids from Royal Navy warships.

The new organisation is built around the formation and sustainment of two Littoral Response Groups (LRGs), with one operating in northern European waters and the other responsible for the Mediterranean/Indian Ocean/Pacific regions. At any point in time, each LRG is to have a Royal Marine company forward deployed on an amphibious warfare vessel and supported by Royal Navy helicopters.

Other units of the Royal Marines are assigned to provide security detachments and boarding parties on Royal Navy warships, protection of Britain's nuclear deterrent and assistance in counter-terrorist operations in the UK.

Commando Force
Amphibious Warriors and More

ROYAL MARINES

40 Commando

LEFT: Exercise Predators Run in northern Australia in July and August 2024, saw Royal Marines of 40 Commando training with Australian, US, and Philippine forces in a wide range of tactical scenarios.
(MOD CROWN COPYRIGHT)

BELOW: Royal Marines of 40 Commando led Operation Polar Bear to Sudan in April 2023 to rescue more than 2,000 British passport holders from the African country. The Royal Marine task force formed at the British base on Cyprus and then flew to the Sudanese capital Khartoum on RAF C-130J Hercules and A400M Atlas transport aircraft.
(MOD CROWN COPYRIGHT)

THE TAUNTON-BASED 40 Commando Royal Marines is designated as the core of Littoral Response Group (South) (LRG (S)), which routinely operates in the Mediterranean and East of Suez.

In the autumn of 2023, LRG(S) embarked on the RFA *Lyme Bay* and RFA *Argus* and began a year-long deployment that saw it sail into the Indian Ocean and then it took part in a major exercise in Australia.

In April 2023, 40 Commando also played a major role in Operation Polar Bear to rescue British passport holders from war-torn Sudan, flying on RAF aircraft to secure an airhead in the African country.

40 Commando also has a role in tactical experiments to help develop the Future Commando Force by evaluating new weapons, communications systems, and unmanned aerial vehicles.

ROYAL MARINES

42 Commando

RIGHT: Putting boarding parties aboard large vessels is a major tactical challenge, particularly if the crew of the vessel put up resistance. Climbing the side of a large ship in high sea states requires strength and stamina. When resistance is expected, boarding parties first try to use helicopters to get aboard suspect vessels.
(MOD CROWN COPYRIGHT)

BELOW: Boarding parties from 42 Commando are deployed around the world on Royal Navy warships, ready to search suspect vessels of all sizes in combat and crisis zones. The boarding parties usually operate in rigid inflatable boats (RIBs) to rapidly approach suspect vessels and then carry out searches for drugs, weapons, or other contraband. A supporting task is providing training teams to allied navies to help them improve the skills and expertise of their own boarding parties.
(MOD CROWN COPYRIGHT)

FROM ITS base in Plymouth, 42 Commando is the Royal Marine specialist maritime security force. It is trained and configured to operate in small groups on Royal Navy warships, Royal Fleet Auxiliary support ships, and civilian merchant vessels under threat.

A core task for 42 Commando is to provide a security company whenever the Queen Elizabeth-class aircraft carriers put to sea. Their job is to secure the ships when they put into port and provide close protection against attack by small boats in contested waters. Detachments are trained and equipped to carry out combat search and rescue (CSAR) operations to recover downed F-35 pilots from behind enemy lines.

Specialist Commandos

ABOVE: Detachments of 43 Commando Fleet Protection Group maintain around the clock security at Faslane naval base, including crewing RIBs that patrol in the waters around the submarine base. They also train to recapture buildings and submarines that might have been infiltrated by terrorists or enemy special forces. (MOD CROWN COPYRIGHT)

ROYAL MARINE units can call on specialist support from other parts of the Commando Force that are trained and equipped to provide additional capabilities in complex battlefield situations.

One of the most highly trained Royal Marines units is 30 Commando Information Exploitation Group, which contains the Commando Force's specialist reconnaissance capabilities. Its Surveillance and Reconnaissance Squadron (SRS) is a dedicated unit, and it is trained to be inserted by air, submarine, or boat, on to enemy-held coasts. The Royal Marines of the SRS have to be able to operate from the freezing Arctic to deserts and jungles.

It also has experts in analysing signals intelligence, aerial photography, and what is termed the 'human geography' of local populations in war zones. 30 Commando also contains the Royal Marines Air Defence Troop, which provides protection against enemy air attack with the Starstreak High Velocity Missile.

Another specialist unit, 43 Commando Fleet Protection Group Royal Marines, is based a Faslane in Scotland and provides security for the Vanguard-class nuclear deterrent submarines. Detachments also escort convoys of nuclear warheads between Faslane and the Aldermaston Atomic Weapons Establishment in Berkshire during maintenance periods.

LEFT: Covert insertion onto enemy coasts to gather vital intelligence is the main task of 30 Commando's Surveillance and Reconnaissance Squadron. (MOD CROWN COPYRIGHT)

ROYAL MARINES

45 Commando

ABOVE: As well as operating in the Arctic, 45 Commando also routinely deploys detachments to take part in NATO amphibious exercises in the Baltic Sea region.
(MOD CROWN COPYRIGHT)

RIGHT: In April 2024, 45 Commando was activated to send troops to Cyprus to embark on RFA *Cardigan Bay*. There they provided maritime security for the US-led operation to set up an off-shore harbour to deliver humanitarian aid to Gaza. The Arbroath-based unit got the mission because 40 Commando was already committed to a major exercise in Australia with Littoral Response Group (South).
(MOD CROWN COPYRIGHT)

FROM ITS base in Arbroath in northeast Scotland, 45 Commando provides the core of Littoral Response Group (North), which is has the responsibility of operating across northern Europe.

At the heart of this role is the mission to help Norway and other NATO allies in Scandinavia defend their territory in the Arctic Circle from Russian attacks and incursions. For the past five years this has resulted in the re-activation of the Royal Marines capabilities to operate in the Arctic winter environment. This was the bread and butter of the Royal Marines in the Cold War, but the skill set for Arctic warfare was neglected during the wars in Iraq and Afghanistan up to 2024.

Each winter, 45 Commando and other Royal Marines detachments spend several months in the high north of Norway, working with local troops to hone their winter warfare skills.

ROYAL MARINES

47 Commando (Raiding Group)

AT THE core of the Royal Marines amphibious and water-borne capability is the ability to operate in a range of small craft, including landing craft, armed raiding craft and RIBs. 47 Commando (Raiding Group) is the Royal Marines subject matter expert in operating all these craft.

It traces its historical roots back to World War Two when Royal Marines crewed landing craft during the D-Day landings and other major amphibious operations. 47 Commando was one of the first Royal Marine units that converted to the commando-role, and it played a prominent role on D-Day, landing on Gold Beach.

Since 2013, the unit has been headquartered at the RM *Tamar* site in Devonport naval base in Plymouth, which has been rebuilt to provide maintenance and training for all the craft it operates.

Made up of more than 100 personnel, 539 Raiding Squadron is equipped with a range of high-tech landing craft and raiding vessels, which are used to deliver troops to land during major landing operations. They also use fast, highly manoeuvrable watercraft to conduct hit-and-run operations on enemy ships and to deliver troops and equipment ashore.

Detachments of 539 Raiding Squadron are routinely deployed on Royal Navy Albion-class assault ships and Royal Fleet Auxiliary Bay-class dock landing ships.

LEFT: A new Commando Raiding Craft (CRC) was introduced to 47 Commando early in 2024. They are painted grey to help concealment, and also have new engines providing increased range – more than 200 nautical miles – and speed – up to 40kts. It also has new cooling systems, mast, trim for better protection from sea conditions and a sophisticated electronic suite for communications and navigation. The CRC has three crew who rotate on long journeys, but the vessel also has space to launch drones, carry payloads and to store a smaller Inshore Raiding Craft to deploy on some landings if required.
(MOD CROWN COPYRIGHT)

BELOW: Operating landing craft, of all shapes and sizes, is a key role for 47 Commando and they provide the Royal Marines with ship-to-shore mobility.
(MOD CROWN COPYRIGHT)

ROYAL MARINES

Commando Support

THE COMMANDO Logistic Regiment is the Royal Marine's dedicated logistic unit, providing essential supplies, such as food, water, ammunition, and fuel, to front line commando units in all scenarios and environments. It is based at Chivenor in Somerset.

Its highly specialist Royal Marines, soldiers and sailors also carry out equipment repairs, emergency medical procedures, and fuel provision. The Royal Marines' Viking light armoured amphibious vehicles also come under the umbrella of the Commando Logistic Regiment.

As a result of the Future Commando Force initiative, the Commando Logistic Regiment has been re-organised to enable it to better support the Littoral Response Groups (LRG), with each one having its own dedicated logistic squadrons. These LRG squadrons have the full mix of logistic capabilities to support a range of operations from amphibious landing, combat missions ashore and humanitarian missions.

24 Commando Regiment Royal Engineers is also based at Chivenor to provide the Commando Force with combat engineering capability. It is a unit of the British Army, but its personnel have to pass the Army Commando course to enable them to serve in the Commando Force. Its two regular, and one reserve, squadrons are trained to clear minefields, remove obstacles from beaches, and build infra-structure to support commando operations.

RIGHT: The Sappers of 24 Engineer Regiment operate diggers and other engineer equipment to clear obstacles and build infra-structure during amphibious operations.
(MOD CROWN COPYRIGHT)

BELOW: Oshkosh tankers are used by Commando Logistic Regiment to deliver fuel and water to frontline commando units in battlefield situations. They also provide fuel for Royal Navy, Army Air Corps, and Royal Air Force helicopters supporting amphibious operations.
(MOD CROWN COPYRIGHT)

ROYAL MARINES

Amphibious Artillery

29 COMMANDO Regiment Royal Artillery is permanently attached to the Commando Force to provide fire support during amphibious operations. Its main equipment for more than 40 years has been the 105mm Light Gun, which can be underslung from AgustaWestland Merlin HC helicopters of the Commando Helicopter Force (CHF). The guns can also be moved ashore in landing craft if helicopters are not available.

The regiment has taken part in every major Royal Marines operation since it was re-roled as a commando regiment in 1962. It currently has five main batteries.

- 7 (Sphinx) Battery (105mm Light Gun)
- 8 (Alma) Commando Battery (105mm Light Gun)
- 79 (Kirkee) Commando Battery (105mm Light Gun)
- 23 (Gibraltar 1779–1783) Commando Battery (headquarters and admin)
- 148 (Meiktila) Battery (forward observation)

The forward observers of 148 (Meiktila) Battery are highly trained in co-ordinating fire support from a variety of sources, including 105mm guns, naval gun fire from warships, and air strikes by jets and attack helicopters. The battery is increasingly using unmanned aerial vehicles to find targets and direct fire onto them.

ABOVE: Gunners of 8 (Alma) Battery were deployed to Australia in the summer of 2024 to support Littoral Support Group (South) during major exercises in the remote north of the country. (MOD CROWN COPYRIGHT)

LEFT: During NATO exercises in Norway in February and March 2024, 29 Regiment deployed a 105mm Light Gun detachment onboard RFA *Mounts Bay* and they were moved ashore by Merlin HC4 helicopters to conduct live firing training. (MOD CROWN COPYRIGHT)

www.keymilitary.com 101

ROYAL NAVY FUTURE

Showing the Flag

The Royal Navy heads to the Pacific

RIGHT: In 2021, HMS *Queen Elizabeth* led an international task group of eight warships and support vessels that sailed to the Far East to establish links with allied navies in the region.
(MOD CROWN COPYRIGHT)

BELOW: Next year a Royal Navy carrier task group will transit the Suez Canal before heading east to the Pacific.
(MOD CROWN COPYRIGHT)

In the summer of 2025, HMS *Prince of Wales* will lead a carrier strike group to the Far East to demonstrate Britain's ability to project military power around the world.

The deployment is the culmination of the Royal Navy's effort to re-build its carrier strike capability by embarking 24 Lockheed Martin F-35B Lightning II jump jets on a Queen Elizabeth-class aircraft carrier for the first time.

The build up to the deployment is already underway with HMS *Prince of Wales* and her air group beginning training in the autumn of 2024.

As well as demonstrating the ability of HMS *Prince of Wales* to undertake large scale air operations, the Carrier Strike Group 2025 deployment will reassure key allies and build links with navies across the Mediterranean, Indian Ocean, and Pacific.

ROYAL NAVY FUTURE

Although the Royal Navy gained a lot of experience in power projection missions in 2021 when HMS *Queen Elizabeth* sailed to Japan, next year's deployment will test new boundaries and build links with new partners. The Carrier Strike Group 2021 deployment took place at the height of the COVID-19 pandemic and many of its planned activities had to be curtailed or cancelled due to the health mitigation measures in place across the Pacific region.

The core aim of the new deployment is to prove the full operating capability (FOC) of the Royal Navy's carrier strike capability, which is defined as putting one of its two carriers to sea with 24 jump jets embarked – including the first Royal Navy F-35 squadron. Additional capabilities will also be added to the strike group, including fully functioning Crowsnest airborne early warning helicopters. This will be the end of more than a two decade-long project to bring the Queen Elizabeth-class carriers into service to replace the old Invincible-class carriers.

In early 2025, preparation for the deployment will move into a higher gear, with the main elements of the task group starting to train together during major exercises off the coast of Scotland. This will involve Type 23 frigates, Type 45 destroyers, and Astute-class nuclear powered attack submarines, as well as support ships and fleet tankers.

HMS *Prince of Wales*'s air group of F-35Bs, AgustaWestland Merlin HM2 anti-submarine helicopters, AgustaWestland Merlin »

LEFT: China's new Fuijan-class of aircraft carrier is part of Beijing's bid to challenge naval supremacy in the South China Sea. (CHINESE PEOPLE'S LIBERATION ARMY NAVY, VIA WEIBO)

HMS *PRINCE OF WALES* CIRCA 1941

HMS *Prince of Wales*' cruise to the Far East next year will not be the first time a Royal Navy ship bearing the name has sailed into the waters of the South China Sea.

For the crew of the modern carrier, sailing north of Singapore will invoke poignant feelings about the ship's namesake from 1941, when the King George V-class battleship was sunk by Japanese aircraft. This action ended British naval supremacy in the Far East and allowed the Japanese to capture Singapore a few weeks later.

Three days after the Japanese attack on Pearl Harbor, HMS *Prince of Wales* and HMS *Repulse* made a foray along the coast of Malaysia to intercept transport ships carrying a Japanese invasion force. On the morning of December 10, 1941, the two British battleships were found by the Japanese and hours later swarms of torpedo bombers struck. Without any air cover to fight off the Japanese assault, the two warships were soon fatally crippled. In just under two and half hours, HMS *Prince of Wales* was hit by multiple torpedoes and capsized. HMS *Repulse* sank less than an hour after the start of the attack.

Out of HM *Prince of Wales* complement of 1,521 personnel, 327 went down with their ship. The task group commander, Admiral Sir Tom Phillips, and the battleship's commanding officer, Captain John Leach, were both killed in the action.

In December 1941, a previous HMS *Prince of Wales* was hit and sunk by Japanese torpedo bombers in the South China Sea. (IMPERIAL WAR MUSEUM)

ROYAL NAVY FUTURE

RIGHT: When HMS *Queen Elizabeth* sailed to the Far East in 2021, a squadron of US Marine Corps F-35Bs were embarked to maximise her air group. (MOD CROWN COPYRIGHT)

BELOW: An air group of two squadrons, with 24 F-35B Lightning II jump jets, is be embarked on HMS *Prince of Wales* for her cruise to the Far East next year. (MOD CROWN COPYRIGHT)

HC4 transport helicopters and Leonardo Wildcat HMA2 maritime helicopters, will also come together to start a period of intensive training to build them into a coherent fighting force.

As in 2021, when US and Dutch warships joined the task group accompanying HMS *Queen Elizabeth*, next year's mission will be augmented by allied ships. So far, Norway has announced it is assigning a frigate and support ship to join Carrier Strike Group 2025. The well reported problems with the Royal Fleet Auxiliary's only solid support ship, RFA *Fort Victoria*, mean that allied assistance will be necessary to fill this capability gap.

New features of next year's deployment will be the involvement of the two River-class patrol vessels, HMS *Spey,* and HMS *Tamar,* which have been forward deployed in the

ROYAL NAVY FUTURE

ABOVE: The Carrier Strike Group 2025 deployment will be the culmination of the project to regenerate the Royal Navy's aircraft carrier capability. (MOD CROWN COPYRIGHT)

BELOW: The F-35B Lightning is the vertical take-off and landing variant of the US-built jet, and it is now in service with the RAF's 617 Squadron and the Royal Navy's 809 Naval Air Squadron. (MOD CROWN COPYRIGHT)

Pacific region since 2021. The first frigates and destroyers equipped with the Naval Strike Missile are also expected to join the deployment. Royal Air Force Boeing Poseidon MRA1 maritime patrol aircraft are also set to join the deployment, providing anti-submarine and surface surveillance cover for the carrier task force.

Next year's mission will also be the first time a major carrier strike group has gone to the Far East since the signature of the AUKUS submarine deal to help Australia acquire nuclear powered submarines, and Britain has signed a deal with Japan to build a next generation of combat aircraft.

One of the first elements of the deployment to be announced was the intention for HMS *Prince of Wales* to visit Japan and carry out exercises with the Japanese Maritime Self Defense Forces. It is expected that the task group will conduct joint training with French and Italian aircraft carriers in the Mediterranean, as well as Indian aircraft carriers in the Indian Ocean.

Extensive co-operation with the US Navy and Royal Australian Navy in the Pacific region can also be expected, particularly when HMS *Prince of Wales* leads the Royal Navy task group into the South China Sea.

This region is the focus of great power rivalry with China flexing its muscles in territorial disputes with Taiwan, the Philippines, Vietnam, and Japan. Whenever US and allied warships enter the South China Sea or sail close to Taiwan, the Chinese People's Liberation Army Navy (PLAN) now routinely dispatches warships, submarines, and aircraft to monitor what their rivals are doing. These 'close encounters' have sometimes involved ships colliding or aircraft nearly touching wings.

So, the arrival of HMS *Prince of Wales* and her supporting warships could potentially stir up a hornet's nest. A counter foray by the PLAN's own aircraft carriers, the PLAN *Liaoning,* and PLAN *Shandong,* cannot be ruled out. This would see rival carrier task groups manoeuvring for advantage, with PLAN Shenyang J-15 Flying Shark fighter jets jockeying for dominance with British F-35s.

Carrier Strike Group 2025 promises to be a memorable event for sailors of HMS *Prince of Wales* and her supporting ships. They will get visit the Far East and be at the centre of great power naval confrontations.

ROYAL NAVY FUTURE

A new class of nuclear powered attack boats will take shape in Barrow-in-Furness in the 2030s to meet the future requirements of the British and Australian navies. (BAE SYSTEMS)

Future Fleet

New Warships and Subs

In the shipyards of Britain, the next generation of Royal Navy warships, submarines, and support vessels are taking shape. The first of the new Type 26 have been lowered into the water on the Clyde and shipyard workers are putting the finishing touches to them.

Meanwhile, in Barrow-in-Furness, submarine production is moving into high gear as the final two Astute-class attack boats near completion.

This is the culmination of more than a decade's effort to recapitalise the Royal Navy's aging fleet of surface vessels and submarines, as well as bring new drone technology into service.

Under current plans nearly £41bn is to be spent over the coming decade on these new vessels, and this money is providing a boom to Britain's shipbuilding industry with thousands of new workers being recruited and trained.

Final Astute-Class Subs

Work is moving at pace at BAE Systems Barrow-in-Furness shipyard in Cumbria on the last two Astute-class submarines.

The sixth Astute, HMS *Agamemnon*, was unveiled in April 2024 at her naming ceremony in the Barrow's Devonshire Dock Hall (DDH) submarine assembly complex. She is the second Royal Navy vessel to be named after the legendary Greek King of the Trojan Wars.

On October 3, 2024, the boat was lowered on the DDH submarine lift into the Devonshire Dock to allow her reactor to be powered up and final trials to take place, ahead of the submarine setting sail for Faslane to join the fleet.

Inside the DDH, HMS *Agincourt* is nearing completion, and she is expected to be moved out of the

BELOW: A dedicated assembly hall has been built by Babcock at their Rosyth shipyard to produce the Type 31 frigates. (BABCOCK)

ROYAL NAVY FUTURE

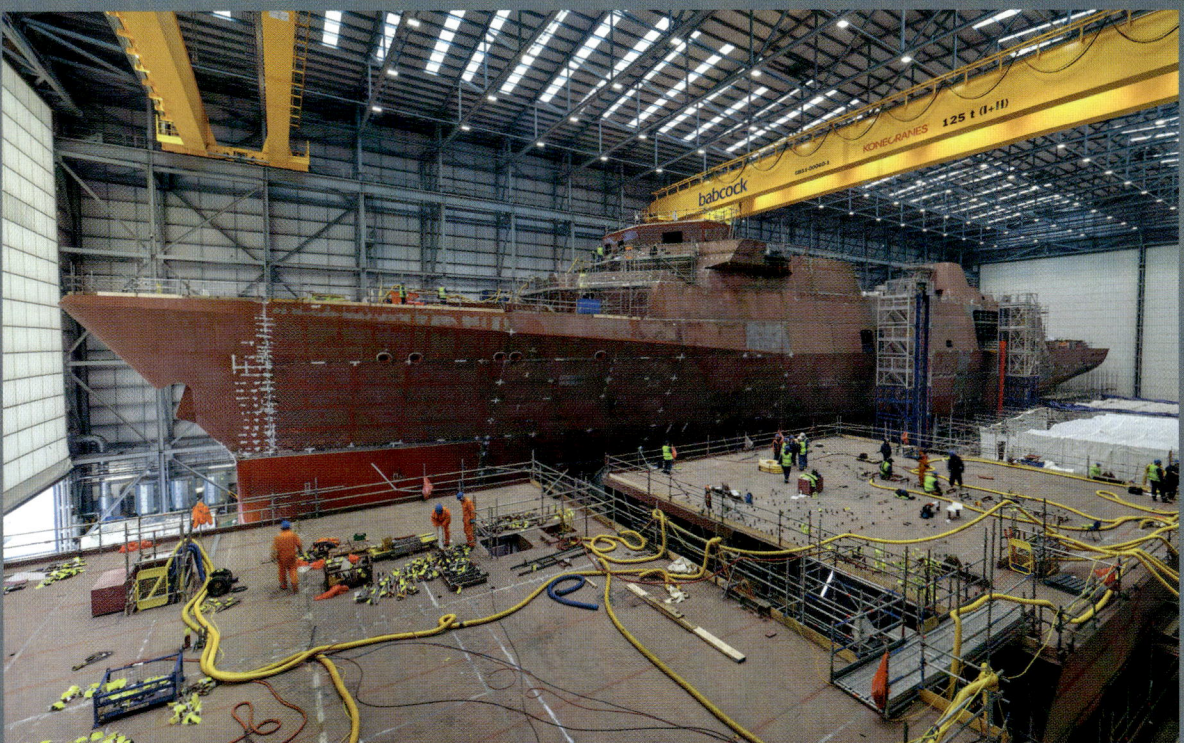

LEFT: HMS *Venturer*, the first Type 31 frigate, is taking shape inside the Rosyth assembly hall. (BABCOCK)

assembly complex in a year's time before being handed over to the Royal Navy in early 2026. Once in service, all seven Astute boats will have been delivered.

As work on the final two Astute boats is wrapped up, BAE Systems are moving to transform the DDH into focus for assembly of the four new Dreadnought-class missile firing submarines. The first hull sections of the new HMS *Dreadnought* have arrived in the DDH, and she will soon start to take shape inside the facility, ahead of completion at the end of the decade.

This is not the end of the story for submarine construction, as work has already started to design the new generation of attack boats being built in cooperation with Australia and America under the AUKUS programme. The British boats, known as SSN-AUKUS have to be ready by 2038 to replace HMS *Astute* when she will be ready to retire after more than 30 years in the water.

Type 26

Replacing the Royal Navy's ageing Type 23 anti-submarine frigates is the service's next highest priority and work is accelerating at BAE Systems Clyde shipyards to bring them into service. The first three Type 26 frigates are scheduled to join the fleet by the end of the decade under a £3.7bn contract signed in 2017.

HMS *Glasgow* was launched in 2022 and is undergoing final fitting out before she starts her first of class sea trials. The ship is scheduled to be in frontline service by 2028 at the latest. Her younger sister, HMS *Cardiff* was moved out of the hull assembly facility at Govan in August 2024 and moved up the Clyde to Glenn Mallan to be lowered into the water, then she was towed into the BAE Systems Scotstoun site for final fitting out. Work is also progressing on HMS *Belfast*, and she will soon undergo the same process.

Work on the second batch of five Type 26 vessels accelerated after the award of a £4.2bn contract to BAE Systems in 2022. To speed »

BELOW: Eight Type 26 anti-submarine frigates are being built by BAE Systems on the Clyde. (BAE SYSTEMS)

www.keymilitary.com 107

ROYAL NAVY FUTURE

RIGHT: The former Prime Minister Rishi Sunak visited the Devonshire Dock Hall in March 2024. The final Astute, HMS *Agincourt*, can be seen in the background.
(BAE SYSTEMS)

BELOW: The sixth Astute-class frigate, HMS *Agamemnon* is in the final stages of construction in Barrow-in-Furness.
(BAE SYSTEMS)

their construction, a new £300m ship assembly facility, known as the Janet Harvey Hall after a World War Two era welder who worked in the shipyard, has been built at Govan. It measures 170m long and 80m wide, to allow two Type 26s to be assembled side by side, under cover. These ships are to be completed in the first half of the 2030s.

Type 31

The second element of the Royal Navy's plan to replace its Type 23 frigates is the building of five Type 31 or Inspiration-class warships. These are envisaged as general purpose or 'constabulary' vessels, and they are not expected to be equipped as 'full-up' anti-submarine warfare vessels. The Type 31 frigates are designed with a large 'mission bay' that can accommodate containers, or mission modules, fitted with specialist equipment, including underwater or surface drones, mine countermeasures kit or supplies for humanitarian aid.

First steel was cut for the first Type 31, HMS *Venturer,* in September 2021 signalling the start of construction in a new assembly hall at Babcock's Rosyth shipyard in Fife. Despite a good start on the five vessels, the programme was badly hit by the COVID-19

ROYAL NAVY FUTURE

pandemic, and the economic shock caused by the 2022 war in Ukraine. Costs have risen and supply chain delays have led to the launch of HMS *Venturer* being delayed. It had been hoped to put the frigate in the water in mid-2024 but this may slip to early 2025, with entry to service planned for 2026 or 2027. The Ministry of Defence and Babcock have both expressed confidence that all the ships will be delivered on schedule by 2030.

Future Solid Support Ship

Keeping the Royal Navy aircraft carrier task groups supplied with food, munitions, and spare parts is the job of the Royal Fleet Auxiliary's (RFA) solid support ships.

The RFA currently has one solid support ship, RFA *Fort Victoria*, but she has suffered from mechanical problems and there are question marks over whether the 1990s-era ship will stay operational until replacements are ready. In January 2023, the Harland & Wolff shipyard in Belfast was contracted to build three replacement ships under the Future Solid Support Ship (FSSS) programme, in cooperation with the state-owned Spanish shipbuilder, Navantia.

The new ships were to be completed by 2032, but the project was mired in delays while the Ministry of Defence worked out how to move the project forward. Harland & Wolff has suffered from a lack of orders over the past decade but a buyout in 2019 signalled its fortunes might be turning. However, in September, 2024, Harland & Wolff's holding company went into administration. Its shipyards continue to operate while a buyer is sought.

The Next Decade?

In 2020 and 2021, the then British Prime Minister Boris Johnson announced major expansions to the Royal Navy shipbuilding programme. This included up to five new Type 32 frigates, a replacement for the Daring-class air defence destroyers dubbed the Type 83s, new Multi-Role Support Ships to replace the Royal Marines amphibious shipping, new Multi-Role Ocean Surveillance Ships and a new royal yacht dubbed the 'national flag ship'.

One by one these projects have unravelled in the face of rising costs and budget pressure on the Ministry of Defence. The national flag ship was cancelled soon after Johnson resigned as Prime Minister in disgrace in July 2022 and then the others were either delayed or scaled back.

All the projects are now on the table in the new Labour government's Strategic Defence Review, which was announced in July. The new shape and size of the Royal Navy's ship building programme will only be confirmed next year when the review reports.

ABOVE: Production of Type 26 frigates is accelerating at BAE Systems yards on the Clyde, with the new HMS *Cardiff* soon to be put into the water. (BAE SYSTEMS)

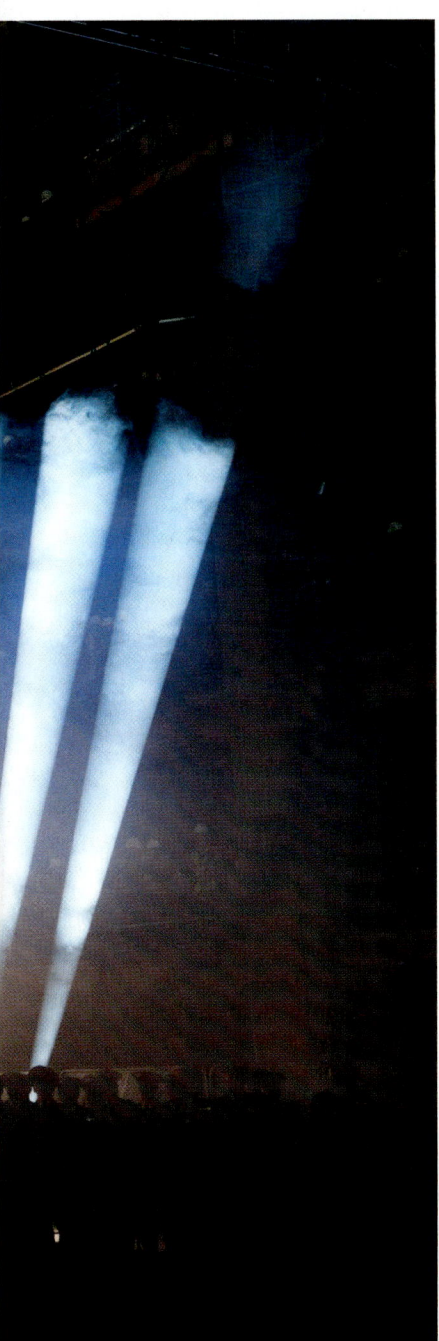

BELOW: The Type 32 frigates are intended to be general purpose frigates to operate in a range of scenarios, from war fighting to humanitarian missions. (BABCOCK)

ROYAL NAVY FUTURE

Stormy Seas Ahead?

Royal Navy faces New Challenges

RIGHT: Dominating the underwater battle space is the primary task of the Royal Navy's Submarine service. (BAE SYSTEMS)

BELOW: HMS *Tamar* is currently on a five-year long mission to the Indo-Pacific to show the flag for this strategic region. (MOD CROWN COPYRIGHT)

For the first time in more than 30 years the Royal Navy has seen its warships engaged in high intensity operations, coming under Houthi missile and drone attacks in the Red Sea.

For weeks on end, HMS *Diamond* and HMS *Richmond* stood guard to protect merchant vessels transiting the Red Sea. As aerial drones, ballistic missiles and robot boats were unleashed by the Houthis, the Royal Navy crews and their allied comrades stood watch on radar scopes and then launched missiles to intercept the inbound weapons. No Royal Navy or allied warships were hit, and scores of merchant vessels were successfully escorted through the battle zone.

This combat has highlighted the challenges facing the Royal Navy in the coming decades. The Red Sea conflict has shown that future naval battles will take place in locations that government ministers and military chiefs do not expect. In the autumn 2023, few military strategists expected that an international naval force would be fighting off a swarm of drones in the Red Sea.

The Red Sea battles also showed the rapid pace of weapon development. Few of the weapons used by the Houthis had been used in action before, so future navies will

ROYAL NAVY FUTURE

ABOVE: Long range underwater drones have the potential to transform naval warfare. (BAE SYSTEMS)

have to keep ahead of a wide range of potential opponents.

At the heart of the Royal Navy's successful participation in the Red Sea operation has been the quality of its people. The crews of HMS *Diamond* and HMS *Richmond* proved their military prowess and their willpower to keep fighting over a prolonged period. Finding ways to generate enough Royal Navy officers and sailors with 'The Right Stuff', to repeat a well-worn phrase, to fight future naval battles is critical to its future success.

The Red Sea operation, however, highlighted other important challenges for the Royal Navy. At any point in time, only one Royal Navy warship was on the line engaging the Houthis. When the tension rose in the eastern Mediterranean over a possible conflict in Lebanon, the Type 45 heading to replace HMS *Diamond* in the Red Sea was diverted to duty off Lebanon. There were not enough serviceable Royal Navy destroyers to do both missions. For the Royal Navy, it demonstrates graphically that warships can't be in two places at once.

All these questions are being addressed in the ongoing Strategic Defence Review, which was launched in July 2024 by the newly elected Prime Minister Sir Kier Starmer and his new Defence Secretary, John Healey.

The review is being led by the former British defence secretary and NATO secretary general Lord George Robertson, assisted by the Russia expert and former White House security advisor, Dr Fiona Hill, and retired British Army General Richard Barrons.

Starmer has promised to eventually raise defence spending to 2.5% of Britain's gross domestic product but has not set a date for achieving this target.

For the Royal Navy, the most immediate challenge is to convince Lord Robertson and Starmer that »

BELOW: The Royal Navy's nuclear submarine fleet is home ported at Faslane naval base on the Clyde. (MOD CROWN COPYRIGHT)

www.keymilitary.com III

ROYAL NAVY FUTURE

ABOVE: HMS *Diamond* returned from the Red Sea in July 2024 after a nine-month long deployment that saw her shoot down ten Houthi missiles and drones. Kill markings were painted on the outside of her bridge.
(MOD CROWN COPYRIGHT)

RIGHT: The Sea Viper missile system received its baptism of fire in the Red Sea on HMS *Diamond*.
(MOD CROWN COPYRIGHT)

it should continue to receive its current level of funding to sustain its force structure, tempo of operations and future ship building programme. When former Prime Minister Boris Johnson set his defence priorities in the 2021 Integrated Review, the Royal Navy emerged as the big winner. For the next decade, Johnson proposed spending £41bn on new ships, submarines, and weapons for the Royal Navy over the next decade. A further £59bn was set aside to replace Britain's nuclear deterrent, which is operated by the Royal Navy. This represented £100bn out of a planned budget of £236bn to be spent on new hardware out to 2032. These are astronomical sums and never has so much money been spent on the Royal Navy.

Starmer's government has said it is committed to maintaining the nuclear deterrent and building the new Dreadnought-class submarines, so the £59bn needed to keep it will have to be spent.

Less certain for the Royal Navy is sustaining the £41bn needed to replace the existing fleet of conventional warships and provide them with modern weapons, sensors and other equipment.

'Nothing is off the table' in the review, according to Healey, so Royal Navy chiefs will have to make a convincing case for continuing with the old ship building programme. The Labour government has already cut winter fuel payments to pensioners to make the point that the public finances have been left in a perilous state by the last government. In November 2023, the National Audit Office watchdog reported that the Ministry of Defence budget was overspent by £16bn and many projects, including several ship building programmes were in effect 'unfunded'.

In this situation, cuts in spending on naval procurement programmes have to be on the table, unless the Admiralty can come up with a good reason to keep it. Starmer and Healey have both emphasised NATO-linked roles over and above the 'Indo Pacific Tilt' favoured by Johnson. So, the Royal Navy top brass will have to make a rapid pivot from giving priority to operations 'east of Suez' to missions closer to home in European waters.

The next major challenge the Royal Navy and the companies that operate the naval dockyards will face is turning around the poor material state of many of Britain's warships. As readers of this publication will have picked up, the majority of Britain's warships and nuclear powered attack submarines have been in harbour over the past year for repairs, upgrade,

ROYAL NAVY FUTURE

or essential maintenance. While some of this is essential 'pre-maintenance' to prepare vessels for next year's six-month-long Carrier Strike 2025 deployment to the Far East, a significant number of ships and submarines are out of action because of their age or lack of dry docks.

One of Britain's youngest Astute-class submarines, HMS *Audacious*, has been out of action for nearly 18 months because a project to refurbish a dry dock to carry out submarine maintenance in Devonport dockyard was delayed in order to save money. When HMS *Audacious* suffered a mechanical problem that required her to be taken out of the water for repairs, work on the dry dock had not even started.

The situation with Type 23 frigates is approaching a critical juncture because the 1990s-era ships are becoming increasingly difficult to keep in service at economical cost. Major upkeep and upgrades are coming at more than £100m a go, yet these ships are all set to be retired by 2035 when all the Type 26 and Type 31 frigates are in service. Two Type 26s are in the water at BAE Systems Govan shipyard on the Clyde but are still four years away from being ready for frontline service. In the meantime, the Type 23 fleet could shrink from its current strength of nine vessels to seven next year as older hulls are paid off. By the time the first Type 26s enter service, there could be less than five working Type 23s. If the new ships are late, the Royal Navy's frigate fleet could find itself seriously compromised. »

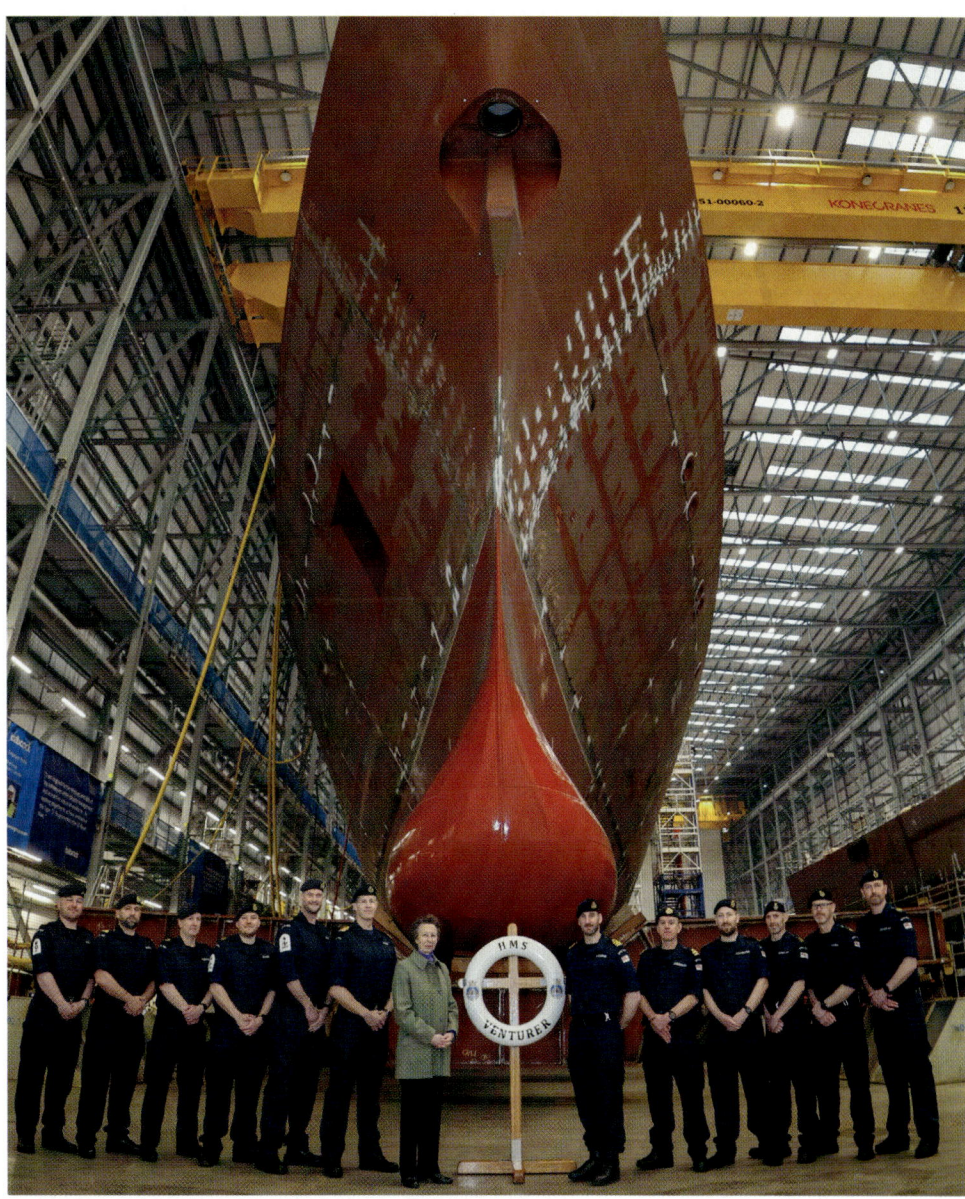

ABOVE: The first Type 31 frigate, HMS *Venturer*, is taking shape in the Rosyth shipyard. (MOD CROWN COPYRIGHT)

LEFT: Spearfish homing torpedoes are the main armament of the Royal Navy's Astute-class nuclear submarines. (BAE SYSTEMS)

ROYAL NAVY FUTURE

RIGHT: In July 2024, the crew of HMS *Diamond* returned from the Red Sea to a hero's welcome in Portsmouth from friends and family. (MOD CROWN COPYRIGHT)

Coming up with new ways to keep the Royal Navy's current ships in the water, at reasonable cost, is a top priority for both the Admiralty and the dockyard operators, BAE Systems and Babcock. This may require drastic action, such as diverting money from the building programme to invest in dockyard infrastructure and shipyard work force skills to keep the fleet in action.

Underpinning all these measures is finding enough officers and sailors to crew the Royal Navy warships and submarines. Recruiting campaigns, such as the current *'born in [insert name of small town], made in the Royal Navy'* are getting young people to take the King's shilling, but more sailors are still leaving the Royal Navy, than joining. The recruiting adverts look exciting, but the realities of life at sea often fall short of expectations.

As a first step in July, the new Labour government agreed to raise the annual salary of new recruits from £18,000 to £25,000 when they begin training. An above inflation pay rise of 6% of the rest of the navy was also announced. This is a good start, but other measures are clearly needed to improve the quality of life of sailors to make them stay longer in the service. Better barracks and improved food, as well as improvements to family accommodation, must all be on the agenda if Healey and his ministers want to address the Royal Navy recruiting and retention crisis.

The Red Sea battles over the past year showed the Royal Navy at its best. The crews of HMS *Diamond* and HMS *Richmond* performed according to the finest traditions of Britain's Naval Service. The Royal Navy is clearly doing a lot right. Doing more of it - at an affordable cost – is the biggest challenge facing the Admiralty.

BELOW: The new Type 26 frigates are to be the Royal Navy's new anti-submarine vessels to replace the aging Type 23 frigates. (BAE SYSTEMS)